The Virtues of Imam Abū Ḥanīfa And His Two Companions Abū Yūsuf and Muḥammad ibn al-Ḥasan

The Virtues of Imam Abū Ḥanīfa

And His Two Companions
Abū Yūsuf and Muḥammad ibn al-Ḥasan

by

Imam Ḥāfiẓ Abū ʿAbdallāh Muḥammad al-Dhahabī

With notes and commentary by

Abū al-Wafāʾ al-Afghānī and
Ustādh Muḥammad Zāhid al-Kawtharī

Translated by Khalid Williams

Published by
©Visions of Reality Books 1435AH, October 2014
www.visions-of-reality.com

First Edition

The book is printed on acid free paper of archival quality.
Printed and bound in the United Kingdom

Thanks are due to:
Abdassamad Clarke (Design and Typesetting)

Andrew Booso (Editing)

ISBN 978-1-909460-05-8

Book Distribution All Enquiries: sales@visions-of-reality.com
www.visions-of-reality.com

VISIONS OF REALITY

Contents

Publisher's Note

It is an immense pleasure to present this brilliant treatise on the virtues of al-Imām al-Aʿẓam,[1] the Greatest Imām, Imām Abū Ḥanīfa and his two companions Imām Abū Yūsuf and Imām Muḥammad ibn al-Ḥasan al-Shaybānī written by the scholar Imām al-Dhahabī.

The Ḥanafī School of fiqh or jurisprudence which comfortably accounts for over half of the Muslims in the world today is named after one of the most outstanding scholars in the history of Islam. Imam Abū Ḥanīfa a second generation Muslim who met a number of Ṣaḥābah, is one of just four Mujtahid Imāms whose madhhabs or schools of law not only survived but gave birth to principles of law that had a profound impact in the shaping of the medieval world.

Imām Abū Ḥanīfa's systematization of Islamic legal doctrine was to have an integral part in the development of many areas of the Sharīʿah and would pave the way for the spread of Islam in many parts of the world resulting most notably in the Osmanlı

1 The quarter of Baghdad where Imam Abu Hanifa's grave is located is called 'Hayy al-Azamiyya' in honour of the Imam.

Caliphate (or Ottoman Empire) and Mughal rule in the Indian sub-continent.

With the onslaught of colonialism over the last few centuries, and with Muslim rule in general decline; events were further exacerbated when the rebellious Wahhabi tribes of the Najd joined with the British agent T.E. Lawrence to disrupt Ottoman supplies to the their army[2]. This resulted in defeat for the Ottomans and for his part Ibn Saud was not only knighted but also made a king. The land known simply as Arabia during the Prophet's ﷺ life and for over thirteen centuries thereafter, became – courtesy of the British – 'Kingdom of Saudi Arabia'.

Criticism of the Ḥanafī school is nothing new but the hostility towards the School in recent times (particularly through the internet in English) has increased to such an extent that lies are now peddled questioning the basis of the School whilst also making spurious baseless accusations against the founder. We hope the translation of this work by Imam al-Dhahabī who was not only an outstanding hadith scholar (and not a Ḥanafī – he was a follower of the Shāfi'ī School) but also a student of Ibn Taymiyya, who many of the critics of Imam Abū Ḥanīfa hold in high regard.

I am also indebted to Sidi Farid Rana for his involvement in this book.

Shaykh Abū al-Wafā' al-Afghānī (1310-1395AH) was

2 These escapades are captured in the Oscar winning film 'Lawrence of Arabia'

a prominent Ḥanafī Shaykh who had studied with some of the foremost scholars of his time. He set up the 'Ihya Al Ma'arif an- Numaniya' a research facility dedicated to obtaining and making available rarer books especially those related to the Ḥanafī School of law. This current translation is based on an Arabic edition of Imam al-Dhahabī's work *Manāqib al-Imām Abī Ḥanīfa wa Ṣāḥibayhi Abī Yūsuf wa Muḥammad bin al-Ḥasan* that the 'Ihya Al Ma'arif an-Numaniya' produced. Amongst his notable students were Sayyid Muḥammad ibn 'Alawī Al-Mālikī who would travel to India to meet him and Shaykh 'Abd al-Fattāḥ Abū Ghudda.

Shaykh Muḥammad Zāhid ibn Ḥasan al-Kawtharī al-Ḥanafī al-Ash'arī[3] (1296-1371AH), the adjunct to the last Shaykh al-Islam of the Ottoman Caliphate and a major Ḥanafī jurist praised by Imām Muḥammad Abū Zahra as a Reviver (*mujaddid*) of the fourteenth Islamic century. He studied under his father as well as the scholar of Qur'an and hadith Ibrāhīm Ḥaqqī (d. 1345), Shaykh Zayn al-'Ābidīn al-Alsuni (d. 1336), Shaykh Muḥammad Khāliṣ al-Shirwānī, al-Ḥasan al-Aztuwa'i, and others. When the Caliphate fell he moved to Cairo, then Sham, then Cairo again until his death, where the late Shaykhs 'Abd al-Fattāḥ Abū Ghudda and 'Abd Allah al-Ghumārī became his students.

Amjid Illahi

3 Taken from Sh Gibril Haddad's work.

Editor's Introduction to the Arabic Original

In the Name of Allah,
the Compassionate, the Merciful

PRAISE BE to Allah, who honoured His knowledgeable servants when He said, ﴾**Only the knowledgeable of Allah's servants fear Him**﴿ [35:28], ﴾**Are they equal, those who know and those who know not?**﴿ [39:9], and further honoured and blessed His friends among them when He said, ﴾**Truly, the friends of Allah – no fear need they have, nor shall they grieve**﴿ [10:62]. May peace and blessings be upon our master Muḥammad, who singled out the knowledgeable folk of his community by saying, **'When Allah desires good for a person, He gives him deep understanding of the religion.'** May peace and blessings be upon his noble, pure and blessed Family, and his righteous, pious, exemplary Companions.

Ever since I first saw al-Dhahabī's words in his entry for Abū Ḥanīfa in *Tadhkirat al-Ḥuffāẓ*, 'I have authored a separate work on the virtues of this Imam,' and his words in the entry for his companion Abū Yūsuf, 'I have authored a separate work on him and on his companion Muḥammad ibn al-Ḥasan, may Allah have mercy on them', I endeavoured to find those works of al-Dhahabī on the lives of our imams, the great jurists of this tradition, Abū Ḥanīfa al-Nuʿmān ibn Thābit al-Kūfī, Abū Yūsuf Yaʿqūb ibn Ibrāhīm al-Anṣārī and Abū ʿAbdallāh Muḥammad ibn al-Shaybānī, may Allah be well pleased with them all and make them well pleased.

Finally, Allah gave me the success to find the treatise on the virtues of Abū Ḥanīfa among the valuable works in the library of the great scholar Shaykh Muḥammad Saʿīd al-Shāfiʿī al-Madrāsī, former Mufti of the High Court in Hyderabad Deccan, may Allah be well pleased with him, one the most valuable libraries in Hyderabad containing many rare books of Hadith and jurisprudence. We took the opportunity of making a copy of it so that we could publish it through our committee, the Committee for the Revival of Ḥanafī Scholarship [*Lajnat Iḥyāʾ al-Maʿārif al-Nuʿmāniyya*].

Allah also gave me the success to find the treatise on Abū Ḥanīfa's two companions Abū Yūsuf and Muḥammad, may Allah have mercy on them, in the possession of our friend Ustādh Muḥammad Zāhid al-Kawtharī, a former scholar of the Ottoman Caliphate. He had copied it from a manuscript from the eight century AH he found among a collection of works purchased by his friend, the late Sayyid Muḥammad Amīn al-Khānijī, a well-known bookseller, from the Bayt al-Saqaṭī in Damascus, Syria. He lent this collection to him in the year 1347 AH, before sending it to the west. This was a gift of good fortune from Allah.

The copy of the work on Abū Ḥanīfa was replete with errors, so we sent it to Ustādh al-Kawtharī in Egypt so that he could correct it and comment on it at the committee's request. We also requested that he comment on the treatise on the two companions. He fulfilled the request most thoroughly, as the reader will see, and then gifted the text to the committee – may Allah reward him well and favour the Muslims by giving him a long life.

Where things were missing from the source text, I inserted passages between brackets from the book *Faḍā'il Abī Ḥanīfa wa-Aṣḥābih* by Ḥāfiẓ Ibn Abī al-ʿAwwām, because much of what is in the source text is taken from it verbatim. I made these replacements without further comment; anything else added to the text is referenced in the notes. The notes of Ustādh Muḥammad Zāhid al-Kawtharī are denoted by the symbol (K).

On Imam al-Dhahabī

Ḥāfiẓ Shams al-Dīn Abū al-Maḥāsin Muḥammad ibn ʿAlī ibn al-Ḥasan al-Ḥusaynī al-Dimashqī said in *Dhayl Tadhkirat al-Ḥuffāẓ*:

> He is the great shaykh, imam and scholar, shaykh of the Hadith scholars and exemplar of the

ḥuffāẓ and the reciters, the renowned *muḥaddith* and historian of Syria, Shams al-Dīn ʿAbdallāh Muḥammad ibn Aḥmad ibn ʿUthmān ibn Qāyimāz ibn ʿAbdallāh al-Turkmānī al-Fāriqī al-Aṣl al-Dimashqī al-Shāfiʿī, known as al-Dhahabī, author of this work [*Tadhkirat al-Ḥuffāẓ*].

He was born in Damascus in the year 673 AH, and began his study of Hadith in the year 692. He studied in Damascus under Abū Ḥafṣ ʿUmar ibn al-Qawwās, Abū al-Faḍl ibn ʿAsākir and others, in Egypt under al-Abraqūhī, in Cairo under al-Dimyāṭī, in northern Syria under al-Gharrāfī, in Baalbek under al-Tāj ʿAbd al-Khāliq, in Aleppo under Sanqar al-Zaynī, in Nablus under al-ʿImād ibn Badrān and in Mecca under al-Tawzarī. He was given *ijāza* by several companions of Ibn Ṭabarzad, al-Kindī, Ḥanbal, Ibn al-Ḥarastānī and others. In his *al-Muʿjam al-Kabīr*, he named over 1,200 scholars who transmitted hadiths to him via direct transmission and *ijāza*. He collected the narrations of many of his shaykhs and engaged in various sciences of transmission including critically examining narrators, authenticating texts and chains of transmission, researching alternative chains for other collections, and abridging the works of earlier and later scholars, as well as authoring many of his own books. One of his longer works is *Tārīkh al-Islām*,[1] and one of the best

1 A copy in 23 volumes is held at the Ahmet 3rd Library, Istanbul. (K)

is *Mīzān al-Iʿtidāl fī Naqd al-Rijāl*, although many of the entries are abridged and require expansion. His authored works, abridgements and collections amount to almost one hundred works in all, some of which have become known throughout the lands.

He was a man of noted intelligence and a renowned *ḥāfiẓ*, and was appointed Shaykh at the Ẓāhiriyya, the Nafīsiyya, the Fāḍiliyya, the Tankiziyya and Umm al-Malik al-Ṣāliḥ.

He continued to write until he lost his sight in the year 743, and died on the eve of Monday the 3rd of Dhul-Qaʿda, 748 in Damascus. He was buried in the Bāb Ṣaghīr cemetery, may Allah have mercy on him.

He took transmission of the seven dominant recitations of the Qur'an from Shaykh Abū ʿAbdallāh ibn Jibrīl al-Miṣrī of Damascus and recited a complete reading of the Qur'an under his instruction according to the schools of the seven reciters, as described in Abū ʿAmr al-Dānī's *al-Taysīr* and Abū Qāsim al-Shāṭibī's *Ḥirz al-Amānī*. Many students took instruction in the Qur'an and Sunna from him, may Allah have mercy on him.

His works also included *al-Tārīkh al-Awsaṭ*, *al-Ṣaghīr* (published by Dāʾirat al-Maʿārif in Hyderabad), *Siyar al-Nubalāʾ*,[2] *Ṭabaqāt al-Ḥuffāẓ* (published twice

2 A copy in 19 volumes is held at the Ahmet 3rd Library, Istanbul. (K)

by Dā'irat al-Ḥuffāẓ), *Mukhtaṣar Tahdhīb al-Kamāl* (known as *al-Tadh'hīb*), *al-Kāshif* (an abridgement of the previous work), *al-Mujarrad fī Asmā' Rijāl al-Kutub wal-Sunna*, *al-Tajrīdi fī Asmā' al-Ṣaḥāba* (published by Dā'irat al-Ḥuffāẓ), *al-Mīzān* (published in India and Egypt), *al-Mughnī fī al-Ḍu'afā'*, *Mushtabih al-Nisba* (published in Europe), an abridgement of his shaykh al-Mizzī's *al-Aṭrāf*, an abridgement and commentary on the *Mustadrak* (published by Dā'irat al-Ḥuffāẓ in the margins of al-Ḥākim's *Mustadrak*), *Mukhtaṣar al-Muḥallā*, *Muhadh'dhab Sunan al-Bayhaqī*, *al-Mu'jam al-Kabīr*, *al-Mu'jam al-Ṣaghīr*, *Kitāb al-'Ulū* (published in India and Egypt with some errors), and *Zaghal al-'Ilm* (published in Egypt with notes by Ustādh al-Kawtharī, may Allah preserve him).

Al-Suyūṭī said in *Dhayl Ṭabaqāt al-Ḥuffāẓ*:

> All scholars of Hadith today are indebted, in the fields of narrator research and the other Hadith sciences, to four men: al-Mizzī, al-Dhahabī, al-'Irāqī and Ibn Ḥajar. Al-Tāj al-Subkī eulogised him with a poem beginning:
>
> Who is left for Hadith and those who seek them,
> Now that Imam Ḥāfiẓ al-Dhahabī has died?
> Who will disseminate narrations and reports
> To all of mankind, Arabs and non-Arabs?
> Who will preserve traditions and teachings
> And protect them from the forgeries of liars?
> Who remains who knows the mysteries of the art,

To help you resolve your doubts and misgivings?
...
He is the Imam whose narrations have spread,
And whose noble students have covered the earth.
A trusted, truthful, well-versed *ḥāfiẓ*
Whose words were more reliable than books.
Allah is Greatest! What a scholar! What a memory!
What a pious ascetic, always aware of Allah![3]

It remains for us to say that this precious work has been published under the patronage of our liege, the noble and munificent King whose grace is felt across the land, his majesty, the Sultan and son of a Sultan, the patron of sciences and supporter of his subjects, the sun of the tradition and the religion, Asaf Jah VII Mir Osman Ali Khan Bahadur, may his kingdom remain ever resplendent in the mantles of glory and progress.

This was written under the auspices of the Committee for the Revival of Ḥanafī Scholarship, in

3 This is what Ibn al-Subkī said about al-Dhahabī when he died, as moved as he was by this momentous occasion. This did not prevent him from expressing his critical opinions of al-Dhahabī occasionally in *Ṭabaqāt al-Shāfiʿīyya*. Al-Dhahabī himself did the same when Ibn Taymiyya died, despite the many criticisms he had of him. May Allah grant His pardon to them and to us, by His favour and grace. Examples of both can be found in *Takmilat al-Radd ʿalā Nūniyyat Ibn al-Qayyim*. (K)

Hyderabad Deccan, may Allah protect it from evils and tribulations, in the sacred month of Dhul-Qaʿda in the year 1366 AH. Praise and glory be to Allah.

Abū al-Wafāʾ al-Afghānī
(1310-1395AH)

One
Imam Abū Ḥanīfa

In the Name of Allah, the Compassionate, the Merciful. Praise be to Allah, and may the blessings of Allah be upon Muḥammad, the best of men.

This is a book of narrations concerning the greatest jurist and scholar of his age, Abū Ḥanīfa, a man of noble rank, pure soul and high status. His name was al-Nuʿmān ibn Thābit ibn Zūṭā.[4] He was the Mufti of Kufa. He was born in Kufa in the year 80 AH,[5] during

4 Zūṭā was not Thābit's father, but between them were al-Nuʿmān and al-Marzabān. Zūṭā's father was called Māh, according to Imam Masʿūd ibn Shayba in *al-Taʿlīm*; this is also authentically narrated from Ismāʿīl ibn Ḥammād. (K)

5 The author chose the latest of all the narrated dates of birth in order to err on the side of caution, as has been the practice of the majority of scholars. But since there is no other evidence to suggest that this is the strongest position, it is worthy of mention that the narration of Ibn Dhawwād states that he was born in the year 61 AH. Al-Samʿānī's *Ansāb* has 70 AH, as does Ibn Ḥibbān's *al-Jarḥ wal-Taʿdīl* and Abū Qāsim al-Samnānī's *Rawḍa al-Quḍāh* (al-Samnānī was a contemporary of al-Khaṭīb al-Baghdādī). This latter opinion is supported by the fact that Ḥāfiẓ Muḥammad ibn Makhlad al-ʿAṭṭār considered Abū Ḥanīfa's son Ḥammād's narration from Mālik to be an example of an older man narrating from a younger, and by the fact that Abū Ḥanīfa was concerned with who should succeed al-Nakhaʿī, which was after he had

the caliphate of ʿAbd al-Malik ibn Marwān. May Allah be pleased with him and bestow His good pleasure upon him, and preserve and give success to what he clarified of the Upright Religion.

Several of the Companions ﷺ were still alive at the time, and he can be numbered among their Followers [*tābiʿūn*] Allah willing, for it is authentically related that he saw[6] Anas ibn Mālik ﷺ when Anas came to

---

become advanced in his study of theology.

Al-ʿAqīlī relates in *al-Ḍuʿafāʾ*, on the authority of Aḥmad ibn Muḥammad al-Harawī – Muḥammad ibn al-Mughīra al-Balkhī – Ismāʿīl ibn Ibrāhīm, that Muḥammad ibn Sulaymān al-Aṣfahānī said, 'When Ibrāhīm [al-Nakhaʿī] died, five of the people of Kufa, including ʿUmar ibn Qays al-Māṣir and Abū Ḥanīfa, met together and gathered forty thousand dirhams, which they took to al-Ḥakam ibn ʿUyayna and said, "We have gathered forty thousand dirhams which we will give to you if you will be our head in the matter of *al-irjāʾ*." Al-Ḥakam declined, so they went to Ḥammād ibn Abī Sulaymān and made the same offer, and he accepted it.'

The *irjāʾ* referred to here is the doctrine of *irjāʾ* within the Sunna, as explained in al-Luknawī's *al-Rafʿ wal-Takmīl*. [Translator's note: The doctrine of *irjāʾ* which is 'within the Sunna' is that which defers to Allah the knowledge of whether a given sinner will be punished or forgiven, and states that faith and action are separate, which was the position of Imam Abū Ḥanīfa. This contrasts with the heretical *irjāʾ* which states that it is impossible for any Muslim to be punished in the afterlife, no matter what sins he commits; Imam Abū Ḥanīfa was, of course, entirely innocent of this belief.]

Moreover, he narrated from several Companions ﷺ, as I showed in *al-Taʿnīb* and as I commented on in my critical edition of Sibṭ ibn al-Jawzī's *al-Intiṣār wal-Tarjīḥ*. None of this could be authentic if he was not born until the year 80 AH. Allah knows best. (K)

6 Moreover, Ibn ʿAbd al-Barr relates in *Jāmiʿ Bayān al-ʿIlm wa Faḍlih*

Kufa. Muḥammad ibn Saʿd reported on the authority of Sayf ibn Jābir that he heard Abū Ḥanīfa say, 'I saw Anas ﷺ.'

Yaʿqūb ibn Shayba al-Sudūsī said, 'Abū Ḥanīfa was [the descendant of] a freedman of the tribe of Taym Allāh ibn Thaʿlaba ibn Bakr ibn Wāʾil.' Abū Khāzim ʿAbd al-Ḥamīd al-Qāḍī said, 'I asked Ibn Ismāʿīl ibn Ḥammād ibn Abī Ḥanīfa, "What is your tribal affiliation?" He replied, "Thābit, Abū Ḥanīfa's father, was captured in a battle in Kabul, and a women from the tribe of Taym Allāh ibn Thaʿlaba bought him and set him free."'[7]

---

that he took narrations from the Companion Ibn Jazʾ, and the scholars of Hadith have compiled several collections in which Abū Ḥanīfa narrates on the authority of several Companions ﷺ. These include the collections of Abū Ḥāmid Muḥammad ibn Hārūn al-Ḥaḍramī, Abū al-Ḥusayn ʿAlī ibn Aḥmad ibn ʿĪsā and Abū Maʿshar ʿAbd al-Karīm, as related by Ibn Ḥajar in *al-Muʿjam al-Mufahras* and Shams ibn Ṭūlūn in *al-Fihrist al-Awsaṭ*; and also the collection of Abū Bakr ʿAbd al-Raḥmān ibn Muḥammad ibn Aḥmad al-Sarkhasī, as related by Sibṭ ibn al-Jawzī in *al-Intiṣār wal-Tarjīḥ*. (K)

7 The 'Ibn Ismāʿīl' in the chain is unknown and lived long after the fact, so what he says cannot have precedence over what Ismāʿīl and the Imam said themselves. (W)

Ibn Ismāʿīl is unknown both in identity and in character, so his narration is not sound, especially given that it contradicts the narration of Ismāʿīl ibn Ḥammād himself as related in al-Ṣīmarī's *Kitāb* and al-Khaṭīb's *Tārīkh*, wherein Ismāʿīl is reported to have said, 'I am Ismāʿīl ibn Ḥammād ibn al-Nuʿmān ibn Thābit ibn al-Nuʿmān ibn al-Marzubān, from the free sons of Persia. By Allah, there is no slavery in our line...'

Rather, Abū Ḥanīfa's relationship to the Taym Allāh ibn Thaʿlaba tribe was one of pledged affiliation. Al-Ṭaḥāwī says in *Mushkil al-*

Abū Nuʿaym al-Faḍl ibn Dukayn said, 'Abū Ḥanīfa had a beautiful face and beard, and dressed well.' ʿAbd al-Wahhāb[8] ibn Ziyād said, 'I saw Abū Ḥanīfa in Kufa wearing a long black cloak.' In Egypt, ʿAlī ibn ʿAbd al-Raḥmān ibn Muḥammad ibn al-Mughīra al-Kūfī said, 'I heard my father say that he saw a shaykh in the Kufa mosque issuing legal opinions to the people, wearing a long cloak. He asked who it was, and they told him it was Abū Ḥanīfa.'

The Qāḍī of Egypt Abū al-Qāsim ʿAbdallāh ibn Muḥammad ibn Aḥmad ibn Yaḥyā ibn al-Ḥārith ibn Abī al-ʿAwwām al-Saʿdī said in his one-volume book *Faḍā'il Abī Ḥanīfa*:

Āthār, 'I heard Bakkār ibn Qutayba report that Abū ʿAbd al-Raḥmān al-Muqrī said, "I went to Abū Ḥanīfa, and he said to me, 'Who is this man?' I replied, 'A man whom Allah has blessed with Islam.' He said, 'Do not say that, but pledge affiliation to a tribe, and then join them; that is how it was with me.'"'

Ibn Aʿyun relates the same on the authority of Aḥmad ibn Manṣūr al-Ramādī from al-Muqrī, and the narration of Ibn Abī al-ʿAwwām on the authority of Yaʿqūb ibn Shayba adds: '...And I found them to be a people of sincerity.'

This shows that Abū Ḥanīfa's affiliation to the Taym Allāh ibn Thaʿlaba tribe was not due to one of his forefathers embracing Islam at the hand of someone from the Taym Allāh tribe, or due to one of his forefather's being freed by someone from their tribe. His affiliation was based upon pledged allegiance, not conversion to Islam or manumission. The conflicting narrations which disparage his affiliation, therefore, are dust in the wind. In any case, piety and knowledge are what is important. (K)

8 Ibn Abī al-ʿAwwām calls him ʿAbd al-Wāḥid, which is correct. (K)

I have it on the authority of Ibrāhīm ibn Aḥmad ibn Sahl al-Tirmidhī – al-Qāsim ibn Ghassān al-Qāḍī – his father – his grandfather Abū Ghassān Ayyūb ibn Yūnus, that al-Naḍr ibn Muḥammad said:

'Abū Ḥanīfa had a beautiful face and wore fine clothing and perfume. I went to him once to ask him to do something for me. I prayed the dawn prayer with him, and I was wearing a cloak from Qūmas. He had his mule saddled, and then said, "Give me your cloak so I can wear it to do your errand, and you can take mine until I return." I did so, and when he came back he said, "O Naḍr, your cloak embarrassed me!" I asked what was wrong with it, and he said it was too thick. I had paid five dinars for it, and liked it very much. Later, I saw him wearing a cloak from Qūmas of his own, which I reckon cost him thirty dinars.'

His Character and Scrupulousness

Al-Ḥasan ibn Ismāʿīl ibn Mujālid narrated that his father said:[9]

9 Shaykh al-Kawtharī completed this passage directly from the words of Ibn Abī al-ʿAwwām, who narrated it, because there were some omissions in the text.

I was with [Hārūn] al-Rashīd when Abū Yūsuf came in to see him. Hārūn said to him, 'Describe the character of Abū Ḥanīfa for me.' He replied, 'By Allah, he was stern in his defence of all that Allah made inviolable.[10] He kept away from worldly people. He was often silent, and always reflective. He was neither talkative nor loquacious. When asked a question to which he knew the answer, he would answer. O Commander of the Faithful, all I ever knew of him was keenness to protect his soul and his religion. He was hard on himself and lenient on others. He only spoke well of people.' Al-Rashīd said, 'This is the character of the righteous!'

Al-Qāsim ibn Ghassān reported that he heard Isḥāq ibn Abī Isrā'īl say that some people mentioned Abū Ḥanīfa to [Sufyān] Ibn 'Uyayna, and some of them disparaged him, to which Sufyān said, 'Nay! Abū Ḥanīfa prayed more than anyone, and was more trustworthy and chivalrous than anyone!'

10 Ibn Abī al-'Awwām's version has it: 'He said, "O Commander of the Faithful, Allah ﷻ says, ﴾Not a word he utters, but by him is an observer ready﴿ [50:18], and this is true for anyone who says anything. By Allah, what I know about Abū Ḥanīfa is that he was stern in his defence of all that Allah made inviolable...' and so on from here. Imam al-Muwaffaq has the same in *Manāqib Abī Ḥanīfa* save that he narrates it on the authority of Abū 'Abdallāh al-Ṣaymarī – Aḥmad ibn Muḥammad ibn al-Mughallis – Ibrāhīm ibn Sa'd al-Jawharī, who said, 'I was with the Commander of the Faithful, al-Rashīd, when Abū Yūsuf came in...' (W)

It is related that Sharīk said, 'Abū Ḥanīfa was often silent and always reflective. His intellect was immense, and he did not converse with people very much.'

Al-Ḥasan ibn Ismāʿīl ibn Mujālid reported that he heard Wakīʿ say that al-Ḥasan ibn Ṣāliḥ ibn Ḥuyay said, 'Abū Ḥanīfa was very God-fearing, and dreaded that the unlawful be made lawful.'

Bishr ibn Ḥuyay reported that he heard Ibn al-Mubārak say, 'I never saw any man with more dignity among company, or better conduct or forbearance, than Abū Ḥanīfa. We were once with him in the Grand Mosque when a snake fell from the ceiling into his lap. He did nothing more than brush it off his lap, while the rest of us ran away!'

Ismāʿīl ibn Ḥammād ibn Abī Ḥanīfa is reported to have said, 'When my father Ḥammād mastered his recital of the *Fātiḥa*, Abū Ḥanīfa gave the teacher five hundred dirhams.' There are many other reports of Abū Ḥanīfa's generosity and largess.

Ibrāhīm ibn Saʿd al-Jawharī reported that al-Muthannā ibn Rajāʾ said, 'Abū Ḥanīfa had a personal rule where every time he swore by Allah about something true during a conversation, he would give a dinar in charity.[11] So every time he swore an oath, he would give a dinar in charity; and every time he spent money on his family, he would give the same amount in charity.'

11 Ibn Abī al-ʿAwwām has a gradual increase of a dirham, and then a quarter dinar, and then a dinar. His narration is very long, and al-Dhahabī has shortened it here as you can see, as he does with most of the quotes in this book. (K)

Abū Bakr ibn ʿAyyāsh said, 'Abū Ḥanīfa was criticised for not frequently mixing with people. They thought that he did this out of vanity, but it was just his nature [to be solitary].'

Jubāra ibn al-Mughallis reported that he heard Qays ibn al-Rabīʿ say, 'Abū Ḥanīfa was scrupulous and pious, and generous to his brethren.'

Luwayn reported that he heard Muḥammad ibn Jābir say, 'Abū Ḥanīfa did not speak much, unless it was required of him. He smiled seldom, reflected often, and frowned always, as though he had just suffered a setback.'

Zayd ibn Akhzam reported that he heard al-Khuraybī say, 'We were with Abū Ḥanīfa when a man said to him, "I wrote a letter to so-and-so in your handwriting, and he gave me four thousand dirhams." Abū Ḥanīfa replied, "If you benefit from this, then do it."' This was also related by al-Ṭaḥāwī on the authority of Abū Khāzim al-Qāḍī.

Abū Ḥanīfa's Shaykhs and Companions

He studied jurisprudence under Ḥammād ibn Abī Sulaymān, the companion of Ibrāhīm al-Nakhaʿī, among others. He said, 'I kept the company of Ḥammād for fifteen years.' Another narration has it, 'I kept his company for ten years, memorising his words and listening to his discussions.'[12]

He studied Hadith with ʿAṭāʾ ibn Abī Rabāḥ in Mecca, and said, 'I never saw anyone better than ʿAṭāʾ.' He also studied Hadith with ʿAtiyya al-ʿAwfī, ʿAbd al-Raḥmān ibn Hurmuz al-Aʿraj, ʿIkrima, Nāfiʿ, ʿAdī ibn Thābit, ʿAmr ibn Dīnār, Salama ibn Kuhayl, Qatāda ibn Diʿāma, Abū al-Zubayr, Manṣūr, Abū Jaʿfar Muḥammad ibn ʿAlī ibn al-Ḥusayn, and many of the Second Generation.

Many great scholars studied *jurisprudence* under him, including Zufar ibn al-Hudhayl, Abū Yūsuf al-Qāḍī, his son Ḥammād ibn Abī Ḥanīfa, Nūḥ ibn Abī Maryam (known as Nūḥ al-Jāmiʿ), Abū Muṭīʿ al-Ḥakam ibn ʿAbdallāh al-Balkhī, al-Ḥasan ibn Ziyād al-Luʾluʾī, Muḥammad ibn al-Ḥasan and Asad ibn ʿAmr al-Qāḍī.

Countless scholars of Hadith and *jurisprudence* narrated from him: among his own generation were Mughīra ibn Miqsam, Zakariyyā ibn Abī Zāʾida, Misʿar

12 Both of these narrations are plainly doubtful, since al-Khaṭīb narrates in *Tārīkh Baghdād* with his chain of transmission that he kept his company for ten years, after which he thought he had learned all he could and left him for a few days, but then returned shortly afterwards and remained with him until he died. He then stated plainly that he kept his company for eighteen years until his death. The correct position is that he first met him during al-Nakhaʿī's time and then kept his company until he died in the year 120 AH. This can be seen from the fact that he was concerned upon al-Nakhaʿī's death with the matter of who would replace him, as al-ʿUqaylī states. (K)

ibn Kidām, Sufyān al-Thawrī, Mālik ibn Mighwal and Yūnus ibn Abī Isḥāq; and from the younger generation were Zāʾida, Sharīk, al-Ḥasan ibn Ṣāliḥ, Abū Bakr ibn ʿAyyāsh, ʿĪsā ibn Yūnus, ʿAlī ibn Mus'hir, Ḥafṣ ibn Ghiyāth, Jarīr ibn ʿAbd al-Ḥamīd, ʿAbdallāh ibn al-Mubārak, Abū Muʿāwiya, Wakīʿ, al-Muḥāribī, Abū Isḥāq al-Fazārī, Yazīd ibn Hārūn, Isḥāq ibn Yūnus al-Azraq, al-Muʿāfā ibn ʿImrān, Zayd ibn al-Ḥubāb, Saʿd ibn al-Ṣalt, Makkī ibn Ibrāhīm, Abū ʿĀṣim al-Nabīl, ʿAbd al-Razzā ibn Hammām, Ḥafṣ ibn ʿAbd al-Raḥmān al-Balkhī, ʿUbayd Allāh ibn Mūsā, Abū ʿAbd al-Raḥmān al-Muqriʾ, Muḥammad ibn ʿAbdallāh al-Anṣārī, Abū Nuʿaym, Hawdha ibn Khalīfa, Abū Usāma, Abū Yaḥyā al-Ḥimmānī, Ibn Numayr, Jaʿfar ibn ʿAwn, Isḥāq ibn Sulaymān al-Rāzī, and many more.[13]

Abū Ḥanīfa's Worship

There are famous reports of the nights of vigil and prayer he would keep, may Allah have mercy on him. Yaʿqūb ibn Shayba reported, on the authority of Bakr, that Abū ʿĀṣim al-Nabīl said, 'Abū Ḥanīfa was known as "the Peg" because of how much he would pray.'

Ḥurayth ibn Abī al-Warqāʾ reported, on the authority

13 In *Tahdhīb al-Kamāl*, Ḥāfiẓ Abū al-Ḥajjāj al-Mizzī lists almost one hundred people who narrated from Abū Ḥanīfa, although he did not claim to have been exhaustive or even anywhere close. Indeed, his companions numbered in the thousands.

of ʿAlī ibn Isḥāq al-Samarqandī, that Abū Yūsuf said, 'Abū Ḥanīfa would read the entire Qur'an every night in one cycle of prayer.' This is a singular report; the more authentic one is that narrated by Bishr ibn al-Walīd al-Kindī, who reported that Abū Yūsuf said, 'I was walking along with Abū Ḥanīfa when I heard a man say to another, "There goes Abū Ḥanīfa, who does not sleep at night!" Abū Ḥanīfa said, "By Allah, nothing is said of me that I do not do." He used to spend the whole night in prayer, supplication and petition.'

Ḥibbān ibn Bishr narrated on the authority of Ḥakkām ibn Salm that Abū Sufyān said, 'We used to visit ʿAmr ibn Murra frequently, and Abū Ḥanīfa would pray the dawn prayer with the same ablution he had made for the evening prayer.'

Yaḥyā al-Ḥimmānī related that his father said, 'I kept the company of Abū Ḥanīfa for six months, during which I never saw him fail to offer the dawn prayer with the same ablution he had made for the previous evening prayer. He would complete the entire Qur'an every night in the hours before dawn.'

Ibrāhīm ibn Saʿīd al-Jawharī reported on the authority of al-Muthannā ibn Rajāʾ that Umm Ḥamīd, the nursemaid of Abū Ḥanīfa's son, reported that Abū Ḥanīfa's son's mother said, 'Abū Ḥanīfa never laid out a bed at night the whole time I knew him. He slept only between noon and mid-afternoon in summer, and for the first part of the night in his mosque in winter.'

Abū ʿAbd al-Raḥmān al-Muqriʾ is reported to have

said, 'If you had ever seen Abū Ḥanīfa pray, you would have recognised that prayer was the most important thing to him.'

Jubāra ibn al-Mughallis reported that a man asked al-Ḥusayn al-Juʿfī,[14] 'Did Abū Ḥanīfa believe in the Resurrection?' He answered, 'I have been informed by one who saw him weeping whilst repeating this verse, ﴾Allah was gracious to us, and saved us from the torment of burning wind﴿ [52:27], and saying, "O Allah, be gracious to us and save us from the torment of burning wind, O Merciful One!"'

Salm ibn Sālim al-Balkhī reported that Abū al-Juwayriya said, 'I kept the company of Abū Ḥanīfa for six months, and never saw him once lie down at night.'

Ibn Abī al-ʿAwwām al-Qāḍi reports in *Faḍā'il Abī Ḥanīfa*, on the authority of al-Ṭaḥāwī – Aḥmad ibn Abī ʿImrān – Muḥammad ibn Shujāʿ – al-Ḥasan ibn Ziyād, that Abū Ḥanīfa said, 'Sometimes I recite two *ḥizb*s of Qur'an in the two cycles of the dawn prayer.'

ʿAlī ibn Ḥafṣ al-Bazzār reported that Ḥafṣ ibn ʿAbd al-Raḥmān said that he heard Misʿar say, 'I went into the mosque and saw a man praying. I enjoyed his recitation, so I stayed to listen to it. He recited a seventh of the Qur'an, and I thought, "He will bow now," but he continued until he was a third of the way through it, and I thought, "He will bow now," but he continued until he was halfway through it. He

14 Ḥusayn ibn ʿAlī ibn al-Walīd al-Juʿfī Mawlāhum Abū Muḥammad al-Muqriʾ al-Kūfī, a great scholar and ascetic who died in 203 AH and was one of the narrators of the Six *Ṣaḥīḥ* Collections. (W)

continued in this way until he completed the entire Qur'an before bowing. I looked, and saw that it was Abū Ḥanīfa.'

Ibrāhīm ibn Rustum al-Marwazī said that he heard Khārija ibn Muṣʿab say, 'Four imams recited the entire Qur'an in one cycle of prayer: ʿUthmān ibn ʿAffān, Tamīm al-Dārī, Saʿīd ibn Jubayr and Abū Ḥanīfa, may Allah be pleased with them all.'

Yaḥyā ibn Naṣr is reported to have said, 'Sometimes Abū Ḥanīfa would recite the entire Qur'an sixty times during the course of Ramadan.'

Muḥammad ibn Samāʿa reported, on the authority of Muḥammad ibn al-Ḥasan, that al-Qāsim ibn Maʿn said, 'Abū Ḥanīfa once stood a whole night repeating ﴾Nay, the Hour is their tryst, and the Hour shall be more wretched and more bitter﴿ [54:46], weeping and imploring Allah, until dawn arrived.'

Muḥammad ibn Ḥammād ibn al-Mubārak al-Miṣṣīṣī reported in *Sīrat Abī Ḥanīfa*, on the authority of Muḥammad ibn Malīḥ ibn[15] Wakīʿ ibn al-Jarrāḥ, that Yazīd ibn Kumayt said:

> I heard a man say to Abū Ḥanīfa, 'Fear Allah!' He trembled, turned pale and bowed his head, and then said, 'May Allah reward you. How needy people ever are to have someone say this to them!'
>
> One day, a servant of Abū Ḥanīfa's opened a

15 This possibly should be 'on the authority of' [*ʿan*] rather than 'son of' [*ibn*], since it is unlikely that the grandson of Wakīʿ could have taken directly from Yazīd ibn Kumayt. (K)

packet of silk cloth, green, red and yellow, and said, 'We ask Allah for Paradise!' Abū Ḥanīfa wept until his nape and shoulders were wet with tears. He ordered that the shop be closed, and departed quickly with his head covered. The next day, I went to sit with him, and he said, 'O brother, what has made us so bold that one of us would ask Allah for Paradise? Only someone who is pleased with his own soul would ask Allah for Paradise. People like us should ask Him only for forgiveness.'

Al-Khaṭīb narrates in *Tārīkh Baghdād* that Asad ibn ʿAmr said:

> It has been related that Abū Ḥanīfa went for forty years praying the dawn prayer with the same ablution he made for the evening prayer, and that on most nights he would recite the entire Qur'an in a single cycle of prayer.[16] His weeping by night was so clearly audible that his neighbours would pity him. It has also been related that he recited the entire Qur'an seven thousand times in the place where he died.[17]

16 The chain of transmission for this report contains Aḥmad ibn al-Ḥusayn al-Balkhī and Ḥāmmād ibn Quraysh, both of whom are unknown, so their report cannot be authentic, especially since the tale itself contains dubious matters. (K)

17 This is not correct, because he did not live in Baghdad but was only dispatched from Kufa to Baghdad for a time, as well as spending some time in jail there. (W)

This was narrated to me by *ijāza* by Muslim ibn ʿAllān on the authority of Abū al-Yumn al-Kindī – Abū Manṣūr al-Shaybānī – Abū Bakr al-Khaṭīb – ʿAlī ibn al-Muḥassin – Aḥmad ibn Muḥammad ibn Yaʿqūb al-Kāghidhī – ʿAbdallāh ibn Muḥammad al-Ḥārithī (in Bokhara) – Aḥmad ibn al-Ḥusayn al-Balkhī – Ḥammād ibn Quraysh – Asad ibn ʿAmr.

Misʿar ibn Kidām said, 'I saw Abū Ḥanīfa recite the Qur'an in a single cycle of prayer.'

Ibn al-Mubārak is reported to have said, 'For a time, Abū Ḥanīfa prayed all five prayers with the same ablution.'

Someone related that Ḥammād ibn Abī Ḥanīfa said, 'When al-Ḥasan ibn ʿUmāra washed my father for burial, he said, "May Allah forgive you. You did not go a day without fasting for thirty years, nor did you lie down at night for forty years. You laid a heavy load on those who will come after you, and you have exposed [the weakness of] everyone else who recites the Qur'an."'

Ḥāmid ibn Ādam al-Marwazī reported that he heard Ibn al-Mubārak say, 'I never saw anyone more scrupulous than Abū Ḥanīfa, though he was tested by whips and [loss of] wealth.'

Muḥammad ibn Aḥmad ibn Yaʿqūb ibn Shayba reported, on the authority of his grandfather, who heard it from ʿAbdallāh ibn al-Ḥasan ibn al-Mubārak, that Ismāʿīl ibn Ḥammād ibn Abī Ḥanīfa said, 'I passed by a rubbish heap with my father, who began to weep. "Father," I said, "why do you weep?" He replied, "O Son, on that very spot, Ibn Hubayra whipped your grandfather for ten days, ten scourges a day, trying to force him to accept the position of judge, but he refused.'"

Aḥmad ibn Manṣūr al-Ramādī reported that ʿAbd al-Razzāq said:

> I never saw anyone more forbearing than Abū Ḥanīfa. Once we were sitting with him in the mosque of al Khayf [in Minā], when a man asked him a question, which he answered. The man objected that al-Ḥasan al-Baṣrī had said something different. Abū Ḥanīfa said that al-Ḥasan had been incorrect. Then a man came along with his face covered and said, 'Bastard, you said that al-Ḥasan was wrong!' The people fell upon him in anger, but Abū Ḥanīfa said, 'To be clear: al-Ḥasan was wrong, and Ibn Masʿūd was right.'

Muḥammad ibn Malīḥ ibn[18] Wakīʿ reported that Yazīd ibn Kumayt said that he heard a man insult and demean Abū Ḥanīfa, calling him an unbeliever and a heretic. Abū Ḥanīfa responded by saying, 'May Allah forgive you, for He knows that what you say about me is wrong.'

Ibrāhīm ibn ʿAbdallāh al-Harawī reported that he heard Yazīd ibn Hārūn say, 'I never saw anyone more forbearing than Abū Ḥanīfa.'

18 Again, it may be that *ibn* here should be *ʿan*, 'on the authority of.' (K)

Al-Wāqidī narrated that al-Qāsim ibn Maʿn said:

> Abū Hubayra took Abū Ḥanīfa because he wanted to appoint him as a judge, but he refused, so he imprisoned him. Someone said to Abū Ḥanīfa, 'He has vowed not to release you until you accept an appointment from him. He wants an appointment, so agree at least to be appointed to the post of brick-counter.' He replied, 'Even if he asked me to count the doors of the mosque for him, I would not do it!'

ʿAlī ibn Maʿbad ibn Shaddād reported that ʿUbayd Allāh ibn ʿAmr al-Raqqī said, 'Ibn Hubayra whipped Abū Ḥanīfa in an attempt to force him to accept the post of judge, but he refused. The people said, "He has called him to repent!"'

Abū Ḥanīfa was once mentioned to Ibn al-Mubārak, who said, 'What can be said about a man who was offered worldly treasures and wealth but refused it; and was beaten with whips, but bore it with patience; and refused to take what anyone else would have clamoured for!'

Muḥammad ibn Shujāʿ al-Thaljī reported, on the authority of a companion of Abū Ḥanīfa named Ḥibbān, that when Abū Ḥanīfa was whipped to force him to accept the post of judge, he said, 'For me, the worst part about my whipping was the worry it caused my mother'; for he was always very dutiful to her.

Yaʿqūb ibn Shayba narrated, on the authority of

ʿAbdallāh ibn al-Ḥasan ibn al-Mubārak, that Bishr ibn al-Walīd said:

> Al-Manṣūr summoned Abū Ḥanīfa to offer him a post, but he refused it. He vowed that he would take it, and Abū Ḥanīfa vowed that he would not. Al-Rabīʿ al-Ḥājib said, 'Did you not see the Commander of the Faithful vow?' He replied, 'The Commander of the Faithful is better able to expiate his vows than I.' He maintained his refusal of the post, so al-Manṣūr had him taken to jail, where he eventually died, and was buried in the Khayzurān cemetery.

This was narrated by Yaʿqūb ibn Shayba on the authority of Bishr, and also by Ibrāhīm ibn Abī Isḥāq al-Zuhrī al-Kūfī on the authority of Bishr with the following addition:

> He was jailed, and then sent to the jailor Ḥumayd al-Ṭūsī, who said to him before he began his torture, 'Shaykh, the Commander of the Faithful sends men to me and tells me to kill them, amputate them or whip them, though I do not know what they have done.' Abū Ḥanīfa said, 'Does the Commander of the Faithful command you to do something which has already been decreed, or something not yet decreed?' He answered, 'Nay, something that has already been decreed.' He said, 'In that case, if he commands you to perform a

decreed execution or specific amputation, then get on with the task, for you shall be rewarded for it.'

Yaḥyā al-Ḥimmānī reported that his father said, 'Abū Ḥanīfa was whipped to force him to accept the post of judge, and he refused. I heard him weeping and saying, "I weep out of concern for my mother!"'

Mughīth ibn Badīl is reported to have said:

> Abū Jaʿfar invited Abū Ḥanīfa to take up the post of judge, but he declined. He said to him, 'Do you disdain what we have, then?' He replied, 'I am not fit to be a judge.' He said, 'You lie!' He said, 'The Commander of the Faithful himself has shown that I am unfit. He calls me a liar; if I am a liar, then I am unfit, and if I am truthful, then I have told you that I am unfit.' At this, he sent him to jail.

Ismāʿīl ibn Abī Uways reported that he heard al-Rabīʿ ibn Yūnus say, 'I saw al-Manṣūr arguing with Abū Ḥanīfa about the issue of his being appointed judge. "By Allah," he said, "I am not assured of your good will; how then can I be assured against your wrath? I am not fit for this." He said, "You lie! You are fit for it." He replied, "Then how can you appoint a liar to this post?"'

Abū Bakr al-Khaṭīb said, 'It is said that he was finally appointed judge for two days [during which no one came to him, and then he made a judgement on the third day] on a single case, and then fell ill for six days, [and then died].'[19]

Abū ʿAbdallāh al-Ṣaymirī al-Faqīh narrates with a chain of transmission:

> Abū Ḥanīfa did not accept the post of judge, so he was whipped one hundred times and imprisoned, dying whilst still in jail. It is said that ten thousand [dirhams] were brought to him and placed in his house, whereupon he became downcast and did not speak. The full sum remained where it was until, when Abū Ḥanīfa died, his son took it back to the person who had brought it, al-Ḥasan ibn Qaḥṭāba, and said, 'Here is your trust.' Al-Ḥasan looked at it and said, 'May Allah have mercy on your father. He was keen to hold onto his religion, whilst other people frittered it away.'

It is related that when Ibn Hubayra heard that Abū Ḥanīfa had vowed never to accept the post of judge, he said, 'He meets my vow with one of his own?' He then gave the order for him to be whipped twenty times on the head. Abū Ḥanīfa said to him, 'Remember your place before Allah, for it is even more wretched than my place before you. Do not spill my blood in vain, for I say *There is no god but Allah*.' Upon this, Ibn Hubayra bade the executioner to stay his hand. Abū Ḥanīfa ended up in jail, his head and face swollen from the

19 The additions in parentheses are from al-Khaṭīb's *Tārīkh*. (W)

beating. Other things have also been narrated about this.

Muḥammad ibn ʿAlī ibn ʿAffān al-ʿĀmirī narrated, on the authority of al-Walīd ibn Ḥammād al-Luʾluʾī, that al-Ḥasan ibn Ziyād reported that he heard Abū Yūsuf say:

> We gathered with Abū Ḥanīfa on a rainy day along with several of his companions, including Dāwūd al-Ṭāʾī, al-Qāsim ibn Maʿn, ʿĀfiya ibn Yazīd, Ḥafṣ ibn Ghiyāth, Wakīʿ ibn al-Jarrāḥ, Mālik ibn Mighwal and Zufar. He turned his face to us and said, 'You are the joy of my heart, and the tonic for my grief. I have illuminated and tied down Islamic law for you, and now I leave the people to follow your footsteps and collect your sayings. Every single one of you is fit to be a judge. I ask you by Allah and by the majesty of knowledge which Allah has given you and which you have protected from the ignominy of being turned to financial ends: if any of you should ever suffer the misfortune to be appointed a judge, while knowing that there is a blemish in his heart which Allah has hidden from the world, it is not permitted for him to judge, and any livelihood he makes from it would be impure. Yet should any of you be forced into it by circumstance, then let him not hide himself from the people. He should offer the five prayers in the mosque, and call out after each prayer: "Who has a need?" And after the evening prayer, he should call

it out three times, and then go home. If he should contract an illness which makes it impossible for him to sit, he should subtract from his provision according to his illness. If any imam usurps battle-spoils, or rules with iniquity, then his imamate is invalidated and his rule unlawful.'[20]

Al-Ḥasan ibn Ziyād reported that Abū Ḥanīfa said, 'If a judge takes a bribe, he is removed from his post [in spirit], even if no one actually removes him.'

THOSE WHO COMMENDED HIS SCHOLARSHIP

It is related that al-Aʿmash was asked a question about a certain issue, and answered: 'Only al-Nuʿmān ibn Thābit, the silk-merchant, knows this subject well. I think he has been blessed in his knowledge.'

Yūsuf ibn Mūsā reported that he heard Jarīr say, 'When al-Aʿmash was asked about detailed matters, he would send the questioners to Abū Ḥanīfa. Mughīra said to him, "Why don't *you* go to Abū Ḥanīfa?"'

Yaḥyā ibn Akthum reported that Jarīr said: 'Mughīra said to me, "Go and sit with Abū Ḥanīfa and learn

20 Ibn Abī al-ʿAwwām adds: 'If he commits a sin between himself and his Lord ﷻ which deserves a *ḥadd* punishment, the *ḥadd* is excused him, because he is the one who is supposed to uphold it. If the sin is between him and another person, however, then the closest judge to him must apply the *ḥadd* to him.' (W)

some jurisprudence; for if Ibrāhīm himself were alive, he would go to sit with him."'

Shabāba ibn Sawār said: 'Shuʿba thought well of Abū Ḥanīfa, and would often pray for mercy for him.'

'Ubayd Allāh ibn Mūsā reported that he heard Misʿar say, 'May Allah have mercy on Abū Ḥanīfa. He was a true jurist and scholar.'

Ḥusayn al-Juʿfī narrated that he heard Zāʾida ibn Qudāma say, 'Al-Nuʿmān ibn Thābit is a jurist through and through. The people of Kufa will never see his like again.'

Abū Bakr ibn ʿAyyāsh is reported to have said, 'Al-Nuʿmān ibn Thābit was the greatest jurist of his age.'

Abū Nuʿaym reported that he heard Ṣāliḥ ibn Ḥuyayy say, 'When Abū Ḥanīfa died, Iraq lost its greatest mufti and jurist.'

Bishr al-Ḥāfī reported that he heard ʿAbdallāh ibn Dāwūd al-Khuraybī say, 'If you want traditions, then Sufyān al-Thawrī is your man; if you want the details, then Abū Ḥanīfa is your man.'

Rawḥ ibn ʿUbāda said, 'I was with Ibn Jurayj when he was informed of the death of Abū Ḥanīfa. He said, "May Allah have mercy on him; a great amount of knowledge has died with him."'

Al-Muthannā ibn Rajāʾ reported that he heard Saʿīd ibn Abī ʿArūba say, 'Abū Ḥanīfa was the greatest scholar of Iraq.'

Yazīd ibn Hārūn said, 'The greatest jurist I ever saw was Abū Ḥanīfa.'

Shaddād ibn Ḥakīm said, 'I never saw anyone more

knowledgeable than Abū Ḥanīfa in his time.'

Al-Ḥalwānī said, 'I asked Abū ʿĀṣim al-Nabīl who was the greater jurist, Abū Ḥanīfa or Sufyān. He said it was Abū Ḥanīfa.'

ʿAbd al-Razzāq reported that Ibn al-Mubārak said, 'When it comes to reasoned opinion, he was the best of them all.'

Ibn al-Mubārak is also reported to have said, 'Had Allah not guided me me through Abū Ḥanīfa and Sufyān, I would have become a heretic.'

Yaḥyā ibn Ādam reported that he heard al-Ḥasan ibn Ṣāliḥ say, 'Abū Ḥanīfa understand what he knew, and applied it rigorously. If he ascertained the authenticity of something attributed to the Messenger of Allah ﷺ, then he looked no further.'

Al-Muzanī and others reported that they heard al-Shāfiʿī say, 'In jurisprudence, everyone is the child of Abū Ḥanīfa.'

Isḥāq ibn Buhlūl reported that he heard Ibn ʿUyayna say, 'I never saw anyone like Abū Ḥanīfa.'

Ibrāhīm ibn ʿAbdallāh al-Marwazī al-Khallāl reported that he heard Ibn al-Mubārak say, 'Abū Ḥanīfa was a divine sign.'

Aḥmad ibn al-Ṣabbāḥ reported that he heard al-Shāfiʿī say, 'Mālik was asked if he had seen Abū Ḥanīfa, and he replied, "Yes. I saw a man who, if he debated you about whether he could turn this pillar into gold, would win the argument!"'

Aḥmad ibn Muḥammad ibn Mughallis[21] reported,

21 He is Aḥmad ibn Muḥammad ibn al-Ṣalt ibn al-Mughallis al-

on the authority of Muḥammad ibn Muqātil, that Ibn al-Mubārak said, 'If the tradition is known but reasoned opinion is needed, then your men are Mālik, Sufyān and Abū Ḥanīfa; and Abū Ḥanīfa is the best of them, the sharpest of them, and the one of them with the deepest understanding of jurisprudence. He is the greatest jurist of the three.'

Salam ibn Shabīb narrated on the authority of ʿAbd al-Razzāq that Ibn al-Mubārak said, 'If there is anyone who has the right to speak according to his reason, it is Abū Ḥanīfa.'

Ḥibbān ibn Mūsā said, 'Ibn al-Mubārak was asked who was the greater jurist, Mālik or Abū Ḥanīfa, and he said it was Abū Ḥanīfa.'

Ḥimmānī. He related hadiths from Thābit ibn Muḥammad al-Zāhid, Abū Nuʿaym al-Faḍl and ʿAffān ibn Muslim. Abū ʿAmr ibn al-Sammāk, Abū ʿAlī ibn al-Ṣawwāf and Abū al-Fatḥ ibn Muḥammad related hadiths from him. Al-Khaṭīb said, 'Some people say that Aḥmad ibn al-Ṣalt forged hadiths. He died in 308 AH.' (W)

Al-Khaṭīb narrates in his *Tārīkh,* on the authority of ʿAlī ibn al-Muḥassin al-Tanūkhī – his father – Abū Bakr Muḥammad ibn Ḥamdān ibn al-Ṣabbāḥ al-Naysābūrī (in Basra) – Abū ʿAlī al-Ḥasan ibn Muḥammad al-Rāzī, that ʿAbdallāh ibn Abī Khaythama said, 'My father, Ḥamd ibn Abī Khaythama, said to me, "Write down this shaykh's narrations, son, for he used to write narrations alongside us in the gatherings seventy years ago." He meant Aḥmad ibn al-Ṣalt al-Mughallis al-Ḥimmānī.' Al-Khaṭīb commented, 'The chain of transmission of this story contains more than one unknown narrator, so I do not consider it far-fetched that it could be forged.' He then goes to great lengths to show the weakness of Aḥmad ibn al-Ṣalt; this is because of the known bias al-Khaṭīb had against Abū Ḥanīfa and his companions. I spoke about this matter in *Ta'nīb al-Khaṭīb* at too great a length to reproduce it here. (K)

Bishr al-Ḥāfī reported that al-Khuraybī said, 'No one finds fault with Abū Ḥanīfa except one who is ignorant or envious.'

Abū Muslim al-Kajjī reported, on the authority of Muḥammad ibn Saʿd al-Kātib, that al-Khuraybī said, 'All the Muslim faithful ought to pray to Allah for Abū Ḥanīfa in their prayers.'

Makkī ibn Ibrāhīm is reported to have said, 'Abū Ḥanīfa was the most knowledgeable man of his time.'

Yaḥyā ibn Maʿīn reported that he heard Yaḥyā ibn Saʿīd al-Qaṭṭān say, 'We do not lie before Allah: we never heard any reasoning better than that of Abū Ḥanīfa, and we follow many of his opinions.'

Yaḥyā ibn Abī Ṭālib reported that he heard ʿAlī ibn ʿĀṣim say, 'Were the knowledge of Abū Ḥanīfa weighed against the knowledge of everyone else of his time, his would tip the balance.'

Ṭalq ibn Ghannām al-Nakhaʿī reported that he heard Ḥafṣ ibn Ghiyāth say, 'Abū Ḥanīfa's speech is more precise than poetry, and only an ignoramus would find fault with him.'

Al-Ḥumaydī reported that he heard Sufyān ibn ʿUyayna say, 'There are two things which I never thought would cross the bridge out of Kufa: the recitation of Ḥamza, and the reasoning of Abū Ḥanīfa; yet they have reached the furthest horizons!'

His Statements Concerning Reasoned Opinion

Nuʿaym ibn Ḥammād reported, on the authority of Abū ʿIṣma (Nuḥ al-Jāmiʿ), that Abū Ḥanīfa said, 'If something comes from the Messenger of Allah ﷺ, we accept it without question. If something comes from the Companions, we select from it. If something comes from anyone else, then they are men and we are men.'[22]

Many people narrated that Ibn Maʿīn reported, on the authority of ʿUbayd Allāh ibn Abī Qurra, that Yaḥyā ibn al-Ḍurays said:

22 This is also the wording given by Ibn Abī al-ʿAwwām, with a very slight difference which does not change the meaning. Ibn ʿAbd al-Barr also mentions this narration in *al-Intiqāʾ* on the authority of Ibrāhīm ibn Hāniʾ al-Naysābūrī, who reported that someone said to Nuʿaym ibn Ḥammād, 'How severely they criticise Abū Ḥanīfa!' He replied, 'The only thing Abū Ḥanīfa might be criticised for is what he said, as we were informed by Abū ʿIṣma: "If something comes to us from the Messenger of Allah ﷺ, we accept it without question. If something comes to us from his Companions, we select from it, and we do not go outside the bounds of what they say. If something comes to us from the Second Generation, then they are men and we are men." As for anything else, do not pay any heed to vile slander.'
Al-Suyūṭī narrates in *Tabīḍ al-Ṣaḥīfa*, on the authority of Nuʿaym ibn Ḥammād, that ʿAbdallāh ibn al-Mubārak reported that Abū Ḥanīfa said, 'If the hadith comes from the Prophet ﷺ, we accept it without question. If it comes from the Companions of the Prophet ﷺ, we select from it, and we do not go outside the bounds of what they said. If it comes from the Second Generation, we debate them on equal terms.'
Similar reports are also narrated by al-Muwaffaq ibn Aḥmad with several chains of transmission, and by Ibn Khusrū. (W, abridged.)

I witnessed a man come to al-Thawrī and say, 'What do you criticise Abū Ḥanīfa for?' He replied, 'Why, what has he done?' The man said, 'I heard him say, "I follow the Book of Allah, and if I do not find it there then the Sunna of the Messenger of Allah ﷺ and the authentic traditions attributed to him, which have been related from one reliable narrator to another. If I do not find it there, then I follow the sayings of his Companions, selecting from them as I see fit. If it gets to the level of Ibrāhīm, al-Shaʿbī, al-Ḥasan and ʿAṭāʾ, then I perform ijtihād just as they did."'

Sufyān was silent for a long time, and then said something that every single man in the gathering wrote down: 'We hear grave words, and fear them; we hear gentle words, and hope for them. We do not reckon the living, nor do we judge the dead. We trust in what we hear, defer what we do not know to those who know it, and suspect our own reasoning before theirs.'

Wakīʿ reported that he heard Abū Ḥanīfa say, 'Urinating in the mosque is better than some analogies.'

Muḥammad ibn Shujāʿ al-Thaljī reported, on the authority of Ismāʿīl ibn Ḥammād ibn Abī Ḥanīfa, that Abū Ḥanīfa said, 'All we do is give our reasoned opinion. We do not force anyone to follow it, nor say that anyone is obliged to accept it. If someone has something better, then let him bring it forth.'

Al-Ḥasan ibn Ziyād al-Luʾluʾī reported that Abū Ḥanīfa said, 'This knowledge of ours is reasoned opinion, and is the best we are able to offer. If someone brings us something better, then we will accept it from him.'

Ibn Ḥazm said, 'All the companions of Abū Ḥanīfa agree that his way was to give precedence to weak hadiths over analogy and reasoning.'

ʿUbayd Allāh ibn ʿAmr al-Raqqī said:

> We were with al-Aʿmash, and Abū Ḥanīfa was also present. Al-Aʿmash was asked about something, and said, 'Give him an answer, Nuʿmān.' Abū Ḥanīfa gave him an answer, and [al-Aʿmash] said, 'Where did you get this from?' He replied, 'From a hadith which you related to us!' He then reminded him of the hadith. Upon this, al-Aʿmash said to him, 'You are the doctors, and we the pharmacists.'

Aḥmad ibn Abī Khaythama reported, on the authority of Ibrāhīm ibn Bash'shār, that Sufyān ibn ʿUyayna said, 'I passed by Abū Ḥanīfa in the mosque, and his companions were surrounding him, their voices raised. I said, "Will you not forbid them from raising their voices in the mosque?" He replied, "Leave them, for this is the only way for them to learn and understand."'

ʿUmar ibn Shabba reported that Abū Nuʿaym heard Zufar ibn al-Hudhayl say, 'Abū Ḥanīfa was very vocal about the issue of Ibrāhīm ibn ʿAbdallāh ibn Ḥasan.[23] I said, "By Allah, before you are through, they will come to us and tie nooses around our necks!" I went looking for Abū Ḥanīfa, and found him mounted on his way to bid farewell to ʿĪsā ibn Mūsa, his face so darkened it was almost black. He went to Baghdad, and was granted an audience with al-Manṣūr.'

Muḥammad ibn Shujāʿ al-Thaljī narrated, on the authority of al-Ḥasan ibn Abī Mālik, that Abū Yūsuf reported that he heard Abū Ḥanīfa say, 'Two groups will come to us from this direction (meaning Khorasan): the Jahmiyya and the anthropomorphists.'

Al-Naḍr ibn Muḥammad reported that Abū Ḥanīfa said, 'Jahm and Muqātil were both evildoers: one went to extremes in anthropomorphism, and the other went to extremes in denying [Allah's Qualities].'

Abū Yūsuf reported that Abū Ḥanīfa said, 'A man should not report anyone's speech unless he retains it in his memory from the moment he hears it.'

Shuʿayb ibn Ayyūb al-Ṣarīfīnī reported that Abū Yaḥyā al-Ḥimmānī said that he heard Abū Ḥanīfa say, 'I had a dream which alarmed me: I saw myself exhuming the Prophet's ﷺ grave. I went to Basra and had a man ask Muḥammad ibn Sīrīn about it. He said, "This man disseminates the tidings of the Messenger of Allah ﷺ."' [Another narration has it: 'This man disseminates the knowledge of prophethood.']

23 He contested the Caliphate, and had the support of Imam Abū Ḥanīfa.

Muḥammad ibn Shujāʿ al-Thaljī narrated, on the authority of al-Ḥasan ibn Abī Mālik, that Abū Yūsuf said, 'Abū Ḥanīfa dreamt that he was exhuming the Prophet's ﷺ grave and gathering the bones and putting them together. This horrified him, so he asked a friend of his to ask Ibn Sīrīn about it when he went to Basra. He asked him, and he said, "This man is gathering the Sunna of the Prophet and reviving it."'

ʿAlī ibn ʿĀṣim reported that he heard Abū Ḥanīfa say, 'I dreamt that I was exhuming the Prophet's ﷺ grave, and was alarmed and fearful that this meant I had apostatised from Islam. I sent a man to Basra to tell Ibn Sīrīn about the dream. He said, "If this man's dream is true, then he has inherited the knowledge of a prophet."'

Ibn Abī Rizma narrated, on the authority of ʿAbdān, that Ibn al-Mubārak said, 'When I hear them speak ill of Abū Ḥanīfa, it saddens me, and I fear that they will incur Allah's hatred.'

ʿAlī ibn Maʿbad narrated on the authority of al-Shāfiʿī that al-Layth ibn Saʿd said:

> I had heard about Abū Ḥanīfa, and hoped to meet him. One day, I was in Mecca when I saw people thronging around a man, and when I heard one of them say, 'O Abū Ḥanīfa,' I said to myself, 'It is he!'
>
> The man said, 'I am a wealthy man of Khorasan, and I have a son who marries women and then divorces them after I have spent a great deal of money on him, so that my money is wasted; and I

buy slave-girls at high prices for him, but he sets them free, so that my money is wasted. What is to be done?'

Abū Ḥanīfa replied, 'Take him to the slave market, and when a slave-girl catches his eye, buy her ostensibly for yourself, and then give her in marriage to him, so that if he divorces her she will return to your possession, and if he sets her free the manumission will not be valid.'

By Allah, it was not so much his correctness that impressed me, as it was the speed of his reply!

A similar report was also narrated by al-Ṭaḥāwī with another chain of transmission going back to al-Layth.

Muḥammad ibn Shujāʿ reported that he heard ʿAlī ibn ʿĀṣim say, 'Were Abū Ḥanīfa's mind weighed against the minds of half the people on earth, his mind would outweigh theirs.'

Al-Ṭaḥāwī reported, on the authority of Muḥammad ibn al-ʿAbbās and Aḥmad ibn ʿImrān, that Ismāʿīl ibn Muḥammad ibn Ḥammād said:

I was uncertain whether I had divorced my wife, so I asked Sharīk, who said, 'Divorce her and then officially take her back.' I then asked Sufyān al-Thawrī, who said, 'Take her back, and if you did indeed divorce her, then you will have taken her back.' I then asked Zufar ibn al-Hudhayl, who said, 'She is your wife until you are certain that you have divorced her.'

I then went to Abū Ḥanīfa, who said to me, 'Sufyān gave you the most cautious answer, and Zufar gave you the answer that accords with the letter of the law. As for Sharīk, he is like a man whom you ask for advice when you are not sure if your clothes were splashed with urine or not, so he tells you to go and urinate on your clothes, and then wash them!'[24]

Muḥammad ibn Shujāʿ reported that he heard al-Ḥasan ibn Ziyād al-Luʾluʾī say:

I went to Dāwūd al-Ṭāʾī along with Ḥammād ibn Abī Ḥanīfa. We discussed something, and then Dāwūd said to Ḥammād, 'O Abū Ismāʿīl, whenever someone speaks about something, hoping that it will be accepted from him, let him be careful not to say anything about the Qur'an that Allah U has not said about it. I heard your father say, "Allah told us that it is His Speech. The one who takes of what Allah has taught him, truly grasps hold of the firmest handle; and if one does not grasp hold of the firmest handle, then what else does he do but fall into perdition?"' Ḥammād replied to Dāwūd, 'May Allah reward you well, for what you allude to is truly vital.'

24 Shaykh al-Kawtharī notes that he saw this story in a volume in the handwriting of Ḥāfiẓ al-Birzālī without the chain of al-Ṭaḥāwī, and with the positions of Abū Ḥanīfa and Zufar switched, and a different wording but the same general meaning.

ʿAlī ibn al-Ḥasan ibn Shaqīq reported that Isḥāq ibn al-Ḥasan al-Kūfī said, 'A man came to the silk market in Kufa asking for the shop of "the jurist Abū Ḥanīfa." Abū Ḥanīfa said to him, "He is not a jurist, but an upstart mufti!"'

Muḥammad ibn Shujāʿ al-Thaljī reported that he heard Ḥibbān say, 'A woman brought a piece of cloth to Abū Ḥanīfa. He asked her how much it was, and she said, "One hundred dirhams." He said to her, "It is worth more than that." "Two hundred?" she suggested. "It is worth more than that," he replied. "Three hundred?" she suggested. "It is worth more than that," he replied. Finally, she asked for four hundred, and he bought it from her for that price.'

It is said that a man came to Abū Ḥanīfa and said, 'Sell me two garments, and give me a good sale.' He asked what colour he wanted, and the man described them for him. He said, 'Will you give me until a week next Friday to get them?' The man agreed. When the time came, he returned for his wares, and Abū Ḥanīfa gave him the two garments and a dinar as well, saying, 'I am not doing you a kindness. I only prepared your wares for you, and then Allah provided them to you, so praise Him.' The people asked Abū Ḥanīfa why he had done this, and he said, 'Did you not hear him ask me to give him a good sale? ʿAṭāʾ ibn al-Sāʾib told us that Saʿīd ibn Jubayr said, "When a man says to a man, 'Give me a good sale,' he entrusts him with a responsibility."'

ʿUbayd ibn Yaʿīsh reported, on the authority of Wakīʿ, that when Sufyān was asked, 'Are you a believer', he would say, 'Yes'; and when it was said to him, 'Are you are believer in Allah's sight?', he would say, 'I hope so.' Abū Ḥanīfa, on the other hand, would say, 'I am a believer here, and in Allah's sight as well.'

Abū Bishr al-Dūlābī reported, on the authority of Muḥammad ibn Saʿdān, that al-Ḍabbī Muʾaddib al-Muʿizz said:

> Abū Asīd, an elderly, virtuous simpleton,[25] used to sit with Abū Ḥanīfa. One day at a gathering of Abū Ḥanīfa, he said to a man, 'Lift your knee, for I wish to urinate,' when he meant that he wanted to spit. The man said to Abū Ḥanīfa, 'Did you hear what he said?' Abū Asīd said, 'Doesn't the saying go: "When you sit with the scholars, sit with a minimum of calm and dignity"?' Abū Ḥanīfa and the others laughed at this.
>
> Abū Asīd was sitting in the street one day when some people passed him by leading a fat she-camel. He said, 'I wish it were mine?' They said, 'What would you do with it?' He replied, 'I'd circumcise it, and slaughter my son!'

25 Perhaps by mentioning Abū Asīd's eccentricities here, he intended to show how generous and welcoming Abū Ḥanīfa was, and how kind he was to those who frequently visited him, even if they were not seekers of knowledge. The gatherings of the people of knowledge were often frequented by simple-minded folk who were not qualified for study, and the way of the scholars was to treat them kindly and bear their eccentricities. To turn them away would have disheartened them; and in addition to being denied knowledge, they would have been openly humiliated. (K)

One Sunday, he got ready and wore his Friday clothes, and put some perfume on, and then went out and sat with a perfume-seller friend of his. They conversed for a while, and then he said, 'Shall we be off to the Friday prayer?' He said, 'O Abū Asīd, it is Sunday today! Some people get the day mixed up, but you get the whole week mixed up!' He said, 'I was sure it was Friday.'

He fell ill once, and Abū Ḥanīfa went to visit him. He asked him how he was, and he said he was well. 'Did they give you something to eat today?' he asked. He replied, 'Yes, some gravy made of sycamore fig and pomegranate jam!'[26] Abū Ḥanīfa laughed and said, 'You are well indeed.'

Al-Ṭaḥāwī reported that Aḥmad ibn Abī ʿImrān told him that Hilāl ibn Yaḥyā told him that Yūsuf ibn Khālid al-Samtī said,[27] 'I sat with Abū Ḥanīfa for two-and-a-half years, and never heard him make a single grammatical mistake, save just once; and even then, the grammarians would have excused it.'

Muḥammad ibn Aḥmad ibn Ḥafṣ, the great jurist of Bokhara, reported, on the authority of Abū Wahb

26 This is what the original says. Gravy (*maraqa*) is made only from meat, while Abū Asīd made it from jam, meaning fruit preserve; but sycamore figs are the poorest of fruits, and jam is rarely made from them. This is just the sort of food that someone like Abū Asīd would desire, though others would not, especially at a time of illness. (K)

27 The chain of transmission here was incomplete. Ibn Abī al-ʿAwwām's book provided the full chain in the section on Khālid ibn Yūsuf. (W)

Muḥammad ibn Muzāḥim (and others), that Ibn al-Mubārak said, 'I did not keep the company of Sufyān until I had first grasped the knowledge of Abū Ḥanīfa just like this,' gesturing with his clenched fist.

Abū al-Qāsim ʿAbdallāh ibn Muḥammad ibn Abī al-ʿAwwām al-Saʿdī, the Qāḍī of Egypt, reported, on the authority of Ibrāhīm ibn Aḥmad al-Tirmidhī, who heard it from Abū Naṣr Muḥammad ibn Muḥammad ibn Salām al-Balkhī, that Nuṣayr ibn Yaḥyā al-Balkhī said:

> I said to Aḥmad ibn Ḥanbal, 'What do you criticise this man for?' He replied, 'The employment of reasoning.' I said, 'But didn't Mālik employ reasoning?' He replied, 'Indeed, but the reasoning of Abū Ḥanīfa was recorded in books.' I said, 'But the reasoning of Mālik was also recorded in books.' He said, 'Abū Ḥanīfa employed reasoning more than he did.' I said, 'So why didn't you speak about them both, turn by turn?' He was silent.

More About His Scrupulousness

Ibn Kās al-Qāḍī reported on the authority of al-Ḥusayn ibn al-Ḥakam al-Ḥibarī that ʿAlī ibn Ḥafṣ al-Bazzāz said:

> Ḥafṣ ibn ʿAbd al-Raḥmān was Abū Ḥanīfa's business partner, and would take care of his sales

when he was away. Once he sent him a message saying that a certain garment was flawed, and that when he sold it he should point this out to the customer. Ḥafṣ forgot, and sold it to a stranger without pointing out the flaw. When Abū Ḥanīfa found out about this, he gave the entire proceeds to charity.

Abū Nuʿaym said, 'Abū Ḥanīfa was always diligent in settling debts, and completely honest.'

Muḥammad ibn Isḥāq ibn Khalaf al-Bakkāʾī reported, on the authority of Jaʿfar ibn ʿAwn (and others), that a woman came to Abū Ḥanīfa asking for a silk garment. They brought it out for her, and she said, 'I am a weak woman, so sell it to me for what it cost you.' He told her to take it for four dirhams. 'Do not mock me,' she said. 'Glory be to Allah!' he said, 'I bought two garments and sold one of them for the value of both, minus four dirhams.'

ʿAlī ibn al-Ḥasan ibn Shaqīq reported that Ibn al-Mubārak said, 'Abū Ḥanīfa was asked which action is best. He replied, "Seeking knowledge." The questioner said, "And then what?" He answered, "Whatever is most difficult for you."'

Khārija ibn Muṣʿab is reported to have said:

Al-Manṣūr awarded Abū Ḥanīfa ten thousand dirhams, and he was summoned to go and collect them. He asked my advice about the matter, and said, 'If I refuse this man's offer, he will be angry; but if I accept it, it will introduce something hateful to me [into my religion].'[28] I said, 'This money has a great importance in his eyes, so when you are summoned to accept it, say, "I would never have hoped that the Commander of the Faithful would give me this!"' He did so, and al-Manṣūr was informed of it, so he revoked it.[29]

Al-Ḥasan ibn Ziyād al-Luʾluʾī is reported to have said, 'By Allah, Abū Ḥanīfa never accepted a reward or a gift from any of them,' meaning from any ruler.

Muḥammad ibn ʿAbd al-Malik al-Daqīqī reported that he heard Zayīd ibn Hārūn say, 'I never saw anyone more intelligent, more virtuous or more scrupulous than Abū Ḥanīfa.'

Abū Qilāba reported that he heard Muḥammad ibn ʿAbdallāh al-Anṣārī say, 'Abū Ḥanīfa's intelligence was evident in his words, his actions and even his gait, and in the way he entered and exited a room.'

ʿAbd al-Ḥamīd al-Ḥimmānī said, 'I never saw anyone better than Abū Ḥanīfa in religion or scrupulousness.'

Muḥammad ibn ʿAlī ibn ʿAffān reported, on the authority of Yaḥyā ibn ʿAbd al-Ḥamīd al-Ḥimmānī, that his father said, 'I was with Abū Ḥanīfa when a man came to him and said. "I heard Sufyān criticising you and speaking [ill] about you." He replied, "May

28 The words between brackets are an addition from al-Muwaffaq's *Manāqib*. (W)

29 Al-Muwaffaq's version has: 'So he was called to collect it, and he said this, and it was passed on to [al-Manṣūr], who then revoked the award.' (K)

Allah forgive us and Sufyān. Had Sufyān been absent at the time of Ibrāhīm al-Nakhaʿī, the Muslims would have been harmed by his absence.'"

Muḥammad ibn al-Ṣaqr ibn Mālik ibn Mighsal[30] reported, on the authority of Ismāʿīl ibn Ḥammād ibn Abī Ḥanīfa, that Abū Ḥanīfa said, 'Ibn Abī Laylā has allowed things to be done to me which I would not allow to be done to a beast.'[31]

Abū Yaḥya ibn Abī Maysara reported, on the authority of Khallād ibn Yaḥyā, that Misʿar ibn Kidām said, 'I studied Hadith along with Abū Ḥanīfa, and he outdid us; we followed the path of asceticism together, and he surpassed us; and we studied jurisprudence alongside him, and he produced the results you can see today.'

Ibn al-Kās reported that Abū Bakr al-Marūdhī said:

> I heard ʿAbū ʿAbd Allah Aḥmad ibn Ḥanbal say, 'We do not think it authentic that Abū Ḥanīfa (Allah have mercy on him) said that the Qur'an is created.' I said, 'Praise be to Allah, O Abū ʿAbdallāh! He has a high standing in knowledge.' He replied, 'Glory be to Allah! His station in knowledge, scrupulousness, asceticism and preference of the Hereafter is second to none. He was beaten with scourges in order to force him to take the post of judge under Abū Jaʿfar, but he refused.'

30 A few links of his lineage are missed out here. His full name was Muḥammad ibn al-Ṣaqr ibn ʿAbd al-Raḥmān ibn bint Mālik ibn Mighwal, as in *al-Mīzān*, *Tārīkh al-Khaṭīb* and *al-Ta'nīb*. (K)

31 Ibn Abī al-ʿAwwām's version has 'cat' in,stead of 'beast.' (K)

Yaḥyā ibn ʿAbd al-Ḥamīd al-Ḥimmānī reported that his father heard Abū Ḥanīfa say, 'Jahm ibn Ṣafwān al-Khurāsānī is an unbeliever.'[32]

Concerning the Evidentiary Value of His Hadiths

Scholars are divided into two opinions concerning the hadiths Imam Abū Ḥanīfa narrated: some accept them and consider them to be valid evidence;[33] others see them as weak because he made several mistakes in them, and not for any other reason.

ʿAlī ibn al-Madīnī reported that someone asked Yaḥyā ibn Saʿīd al-Qaṭṭān about Abū Ḥanīfa's narrations of Hadith, and he replied, 'He was not a scholar of Hadith.'[34]

32 As for the report that he said to him, 'Get out, unbeliever,' I have not seen a complete chain of transmission for it; although Jahm was certainly guilty of heresies which amount to unbelief. (K)

33 This is the opinion of the majority of diligent jurists and Hadith scholars, as opposed to the extremist anthropomorphists. The second opinion is held only by the dregs of the ignorant anthropomorphists among the extremist narrators, whose words are worthless. Just observe how Ibn ʿAdī, author of *al-Kāmil*, unjustly and maliciously criticises Imam Abū Ḥanīfa for forged hadiths which were attributed to him by Ibn ʿAdī's own shaykh, Abbāʾ ibn Jaʿfar. I spoke about this at length in *Taʾnīb al-Khaṭīb*. (K)

34 The chain of transmission for this report, as given in al-Khaṭīb's *Tārīkh*, contains Ibn Ḥayyūyah, who was a weak and lax narrator who would transmit books which he himself had not read under the

I say that the Imam did not direct his efforts to the minutia of wordings and chains of transmission, but rather directed it to the Qur'an and jurisprudence.[35]

---

tutelage of any narrator. A chain like this is not enough to prove that Ibn al-Madīnī said anything. Indeed, Ibn al-Madīnī himself did not escape criticism from other narrators, with one evensaying about him:
Ah, Ibn al-Madīnī, who was offered the world,
And so gave away his religion to get it!
It is true that Abū Ḥanīfa was not someone who was devoted exclusively to narration or holding circles of Hadith transmission. His circles were circles of jurisprudence attended by the most intelligent jurists who were adept at deriving rulings from narrations, and the greatest of *mujtahids* whom he himself trained, and he would occasionally give them narrations, if circumstance required it. For them, a 'scholar of Hadith' is someone who spends all his time engaged in narration without concerning himself with applying jurisprudential methodology to his narrations. Now what is the teaching and application of the jurisprudential comprehension of Islam, compared with bare narration? (K)

35 Al-Dhahabī was not completely accurate here, due to the influence of the errant anthropomorphists with whom he mixed, who were far from possessing a sound understanding of the details and great breadth of Abū Ḥanīfa's knowledge. It could not be that a *mujtahid*, whom half the Muslim community follows (if not two thirds of them), and whose scholarly foundations have been a guide for the entire community for centuries, was ignorant of the minutia of a hadith, both the chain and the text, especially when he lived so near to the time of al-Muṣṭafā ﷺ. But caprice can make a reliable, sound narrator into a weak and error-prone one!
Now what is a specialist in *ijtihād* surrounded by the greatest of *mujtahids*, who themselves trained under him, compared to a specialist in judgement, recitation or asceticism? For such a man, *ijtihād* must involve proficiency in Qur'an, Sunna and tradition, as well as the areas of consensus and dispute. Abū Ḥanīfa's only sin was that most of the

This is true of anyone who specialises in one art: they are less proficient in others.

For the same reason, the scholars have attributed weakness to the hadiths narrated by many imams of recitation such as Ḥafṣ and Qālūn, many jurists such as Ibn Abī Laylā and ʿUthmān al-Battī, many ascetics such as Farqad al-Sabakhī and Shaqīq al-Balkhī, and many grammarians. This is not because of any weakness in the man's trustworthiness, but because he was not an expert in the science of Hadith. He was far too noble to be suspected of dishonesty.

According to Ṣāliḥ ibn Muḥammad Jazara and others, Ibn Maʿīn said, 'Abū Ḥanīfa is a trusted narrator [*thiqa*].'

Aḥmad ibn Muḥammad ibn al-Qāsim ibn Muḥriz reported that Yaḥyā ibn Maʿīn said, 'There is no fault in him.'[36]

---

judges who caused difficulties for the narrators during the time of al-Maʾmūn were followers of his school, and so they got their revenge by disparaging their Imam! May Allah forgive them. The details of this are given in *al-Taʾnīb.* (K)

36 Al-Khaṭīb reported, on the authority of Ibn Rizq – Aḥmad ibn ʿAlī ibn ʿAmr ibn Ḥubaysh al-Rāzī – Muḥammad ibn Aḥmad ibn ʿIṣām – Muḥammad ibn Saʿd al-ʿAwfī, that Yaḥyā ibn Maʿīn said, 'Abū Ḥanīfa was a trusted narrator, who only narrated what he had memorised, and never narrated what he had not memorised.' This is enough to refute those who accuse him of lacking exactitude.

Ibn ʿAbd al-Barr also narrated, with his chain of transmission, that Ibn Maʿīn said of Abū Ḥanīfa, 'He is a trusted narrator, and I have never heard anyone call him weak.' This indicates that the accusations of weakness levelled against him only began after Ibn Maʿīn's time, arising with the evil of the anthropomorphists who were far from

Abū Dāwūd al-Sijistānī said, 'May Allah have mercy on Mālik; he was an imam. May Allah have mercy on Abū Ḥanīfa; he was an imam.'

Some Stories About Him

Al-Khatīb narrated, on the authority of Aḥmad ibn ʿAṭiyya – al-Ḥasan ibn al-Rabīʿ – Qays ibn al-Rabīʿ, that Abū Ḥanīfa used to send his wares to Baghdad and buy goods with the proceeds, which would then be sent to Kufa. The profits would be brought to him annually, and he would spend them on the needs of the Hadith narrators, and their provisions, clothing [and all their needs],[37] and then take it all to them and say, 'Praise no one but Allah, for I have not given anything to you from my own possessions, but only shared Allah's blessings with you.'[38]

Many tales have been told about Abū Ḥanīfa's generosity and the efforts he made on behalf of his students such as Abū Yūsuf and others.

Muḥammad ibn ʿAlī ibn ʿAffān al-ʿĀmirī reported, on the authority of Namir ibn Ḥaddād, that Abū Yūsuf said:

---

possessing understanding. (K)

37 The addition is from *Tārīkh Baghdād*. (W)

38 *Tārīkh Baghdād* adds: 'These are the profits of your wares, because by Allah, they were destined by Allah to come to you through my hands. The provision Allah appoints is under His control alone.' (W)

Al-Manṣūr summoned Abū Ḥanīfa, and al-Rabīʿ al-Ḥāfiẓ (who hated Abū Ḥanīfa) said, 'O Commander of the Faithful, this man disagrees with your grandfather Ibn ʿAbbās. He used to say that if one swears an oath and then adds an exception to it after a day or two, the exception is valid; but this man says the exception is not valid unless it comes right after the oath!'

Abū Ḥanīfa said, 'O Commander of the Faithful, al-Rabīʿ claims that your own soldiers are not under your allegiance!' He asked how this could be. Abū Ḥanīfa said, 'They swear allegiance to you, and then go home and add an exception to it so that their oaths are invalidated.' Al-Manṣūr laughed and said, 'Rabīʿ, do not challenge Abū Ḥanīfa!'

Yaḥyā ibn ʿAbd al-Ḥamīd al-Ḥimmānī reported that he heard Ibn al-Mubārak say, 'I saw al-Ḥasan ibn ʿUmāra take hold of Abū Ḥanīfa's bridle and say, "By Allah, we have never known any scholar of jurisprudence more thorough, patient or better prepared to answer than you. You are the undisputed master of all jurists in your time. They only speak ill of you because of envy."'

Sufyān ibn Wakīʿ reported that he heard his father say:

I went to visit Abū Ḥanīfa and found him with his head bowed, engrossed in thought. He asked me where I had come from, and I told him I had come from Sharīk. He then recited:

If they envy me, then I do not blame them,
For people of virtue have been envied before me;
I will remain as I am, and they as they are,
And most of us will die of anger at their fate.

Abū Ḥanīfa's Death

It is said that al-Manṣūr continued to hold a grudge against Abū Ḥanīfa because of how he had supported Ibrāhīm ibn ʿAbdallāh against al-Manṣūr. Abū Jaʿfar [al-Manṣūr] could not let things lie; he was both tyrannical and proud. Bishr ibn al-Walīd said that Abū Ḥanīfa died in jail in Baghdad, and was buried in the Khayzurān cemetry.

Aḥmad ibn Qāsim al-Birtī narrated on the authority of Bishr ibn al-Walīd that Abū Yūsuf said, 'Abū Ḥanīfa died on the fifteenth of Shawwāl in the year 150 AH.'

Al-Wāqidī and others said that Abū Ḥanīfa died in Rajab in the year 150 AH at the age of seventy.

Abū Ḥassān al-Ziyādī and Yaʿqūb ibn Shayba said, 'He died in Rajab in the year 150 AH.'

Others say that he died in Shaʿbān, but Rajab is more authentic.

We have heard that al-Manṣūr had him poisoned to death, in which case he died a martyr. May Allah have mercy on him.

Some Hadiths He Narrated

We have it on the authority of Abū al-Maʿālī Aḥmad ibn Ishāq ibn Muḥammad ibn al-Muʾayyad al-Hamdānī (in Egypt) – Abū al-Qāsim al-Mubārak ibn Abī al-Jūd (in Baghdad) – Aḥmad ibn Abī Ghālib al-Zāhid – Abū al-Qāsim ʿAbd al-ʿAzīz ibn ʿAlī al-Anmāṭī – Abū al-Ṭāhir al-Mukhalliṣ Muḥammad ibn ʿAbd al-Raḥmān al-Dhahabī (d. 393 AH) – Abū Ḥāmid Muḥammad ibn Hārūn al-Ḥaḍramī – Isḥāq ibn Abī Isrāʾīl – Abū Yūsuf – **Abū Ḥanīfa** – ʿAlqama ibn Marthad – Sulaymān ibn Burayda, that his father [Burayda] said:

Māʿiz ibn Mālik came to the Messenger of Allah ﷺ and confessed that he had committed adultery. He sent him away. He came back and confessed to adultery again, but he sent him away. He came back and confessed to adultery again, but he sent him away. The fourth time he returned, he ﷺ asked his people about him, saying, 'Do you suspect that his mind is impaired in any way?' They said no. So he commanded that he be stoned, and the stoning was performed in a place containing few rocks, so that it took a long time for him to die. He ran over to a place where there were more rocks, and the people followed him and stoned him until he died.

The Messenger of Allah ﷺ was told of what had happened and what he had done, and he said, 'If only you had let him go!' His family then asked the Messenger of Allah ﷺ for permission to bury him and pray the funeral prayer for him, and he gave them permission to do so, saying, 'His repentance was so great that it could have been divided among many people, and accepted from them.'

We have it on the authority of al-ʿAbbās ibn Aḥmad ibn ʿAbd al-Raḥmān, Abū al-Fidāʾ Ismāʿīl ibn ʿAbd al-Raḥmān and Abū ʿAbd Allāh Muḥammad ibn Khāzim (all of the Ḥanbalī school), who all heard it from Abū al-Qāsim al-Ḥusayn ibn Hibat Allāh al-Taghlibī (Abū al-Fidāʾ also heard it from Abū Muḥammad ibn Qudāma) – Abū al-Makārim ʿAbd al-Wāḥid ibn Muḥammad ibn Hilāl – Abū al-Faḍl ʿAbd al-Karīm ibn al-Muʾammal al-Kafarṭābī (in person in the year 492 AH) – ʿAbd al-Raḥmān ibn ʿUthmān al-Tamīmī – Khaythama ibn Sulaymān al-Qurashī (in Damascus) – Isḥāq ibn Sayyār (in Nusaybin) – ʿUbayd Allāh ibn Mūsā – **Abū Ḥanīfa** – Nāfiʿ that Ibn ʿUmar said, 'The Messenger of Allah ﷺ forbade the *mutʿa* marriage on the day of Khaybar.'

Some Dreams Giving Glad Tidings of Abū Ḥanīfa

Al-Qāsim ibn Ghassān al-Qāḍī narrated on the authority of his father that Abū Nuʿaym said:

> I went to see al-Ḥasan ibn Ṣāliḥ on the day his brother died, and found him asking a man

for something to eat, and laughing. I said, 'You will bury your brother ʿAlī tomorrow, and yet you are laughing now at the day's end?' He replied, 'My brother need fear no harm.' I said, 'How do you know this?' He said, 'I went to see him and asked him how he was, and he said, (With those whom Allah has graced: the prophets and the sages and the martyrs and the righteous; most excellent companions are they!) [4:64]. I thought he was reciting the verse, so I said, "O brother, how are you?" He said, (With those whom Allah has graced…), repeating the verse. I said, "Are you reciting, or can you see something?" He said, "Can you not see what I can see?" I said, "No, what can you see?" "Indeed," he said, raising his hand, "Allah's Prophet Muḥammad ﷺ is here smiling at me and giving me tidings of Paradise; and the angels are here with him too, green garments of silk and brocade in their hands; and the houris are here as well, decked out in their finery and waiting for me to come to them." He said this, and then he died, may Allah have mercy on him. Why, then, should I grieve for him, when he has gone on to such bliss?'

A few days later, I went to al-Ḥasan ibn Ṣāliḥ. When he saw me, he said, 'O Abū Nuʿaym! Do you know, I saw my brother last night in my sleep, as though he had come to me. He was wearing green clothes. "O brother," I said to him, "didn't you die?" He said, "Indeed I did." I said, "Then what are these clothes you are wearing?" He said, "Green garments of silk and brocade; similar ones await you here with me, brother." I said, "What has your Lord done with you?" He said, "He has forgiven me, and He boasts of me and of Abū Ḥanīfa t to His angels." I said, "Abū Ḥanīfa al-Nuʿmān ibn Thābit?" He said yes. I said, "And what is his station?" He said, "We are neighbours in the Highest of Heights."'

[Al-Qāsim added that his father said, 'From then on, whenever Abū Nuʿaym spoke of Abū Ḥanīfa or heard mention of him, he would say, "Ah, in the Highest of Heights!"']

Abū Bishr al-Dūlābī reported, on the authority of Aḥmad ibn al-Qāsim al-Birtī, that Abū ʿAlī Aḥmad ibn Muḥammad ibn Abī Rajāʾ heard his father say:

I saw Muḥammad ibn al-Ḥasan in a dream. I said to him, 'Unto what have you passed on?' He said, 'I have been forgiven.' I said, 'On what account?' He said, 'It was said to me, "We only placed this knowledge in you because We had forgiven you."'

I asked him what had happened to Abū Yūsuf, and he said, 'He is one level above us.' I asked about Abū Ḥanīfa, and he said, 'In the Highest of Heights.'

Muḥammad ibn Ḥammād al-Miṣṣīṣī Mawlā Banī Hāshim reported, on the authority of Ibrāhīm ibn

Wāqid, that al-Muṭṭalib ibn Ziyād reported that Jaʿfar ibn al-Ḥasan said in his presence, 'I saw Abū Ḥanīfa in a dream. I said to him, "What has Allah done with you, Abū Ḥanīfa?" He said, "He has forgiven me." I said, "On account of your knowledge?" He said, "Ah, how damaging a legal opinion is to the one who issues it!" I said, "Then on what account?" He said, "On account of the things people said about me which He knew I was innocent of."'

Muḥammad ibn Ḥammād also reported, on the authority of Muḥammad ibn Ibrāhīm al-Laythī, that Ḥusayn al-Juʿfī reported that ʿAbbād al-Tammār said, 'I saw Abū Ḥanīfa in a dream. I said to him, "Unto what have you passed on?" He said, "Unto the vastness of His mercy." I said, "On account of knowledge?" He said, "What an idea! Knowledge has its conditions, and its blights, and few escape them." I said, "Then on what account?" He said, "On account of the things people said about me of which I was innocent."'

Allah knows best.

Two

Imam Abū Yūsuf

In the Name of Allah, the Compassionate, the Merciful. Praise be to Allah, who is Just with His decrees, Generous with His blessings, and Sublime in His glory. May Allah bless Muḥammad, the noblest of His prophets, and give him abundant peace until the day all shall meet Him.

This is a biography of Imam Abū Yūsuf al-Qāḍī Yaʿqūb ibn Ibrāhīm ibn Ḥabīb ibn Khunays[39] ibn Saʿd ibn Baḥīr ibn Muʿāwiya al-Anṣārī. Saʿd was presented to the Prophet ﷺ at Uḥud, but he said he was too young to fight, although he did go on to fight at the Battle of the Trench and others after it. Saʿd was the son of Ḥabta, who was the daughter of Khawwāṭ ibn Baḥīr al-Anṣārī. Saʿd was of the Bujayra clan, and was an ally of the Helpers rather than being one of them. Among his sons were al-Nuʿmān ibn Saʿd, who narrated from ʿAlī رضي الله عنه, and his brother Khunays ibn Saʿd.

39 Al-Ṭaḥāwī has this as well, but Ibn Abī al-ʿAwwām looked into the matter and determined that Khunays was actually the brother of Ḥabīb and not his father, and is hence not in the direct line of Abū Yūsuf; Wakīʿ al-Qāḍī also affirmed this. (K)

Abū Yūsuf was born in the year 113 AH in Kufa.[40] He studied under several of the Second Generation, taking instruction from Hishām ibn ʿUrwa, Yaḥyā ibn Saʿīd, al-Aʿmash, Yazīd ibn Abī Ziyād, ʿAṭāʾ ibn al-Sāʾib, ʿUbayd Allāh ibn ʿAmr Abī Isḥāq al-Shaybānī, Ḥajjāj ibn Arṭah, and others from their generation.[41]

40 This is what al-Ṭaḥawī said, and most scholars followed it, preferring the latest of the narrated birth dates by way of erring on the side of caution. However, Abū al-Qāsim ʿAlī ibn Muḥammad al-Simnānī (d. 499 AH) says in *Rawḍat al-Quḍāh*: 'Abū Yūsuf died at the age of eighty-nine, though this is disputed.' Ibn Faḍl Allāh al-ʿUmarī says the same in *Masālik al-Abṣār*. This would make his year of birth 93 AH; as you can see, there is a large discrepancy between the two dates. It may be that his date of birth was written in a manuscript as '93', but the 9 was partially erased so it looked like a 1, and the reader then read the date as 13; and since he could not have been born so early, he assumed that it meant 113 and that the first 1 had been left off, as is often done with decimals signifying centuries when there is little chance of the reader making an error. Thus the year 113 began to be given as his birth date in most books, the authors mistakenly thinking this to be a correction of the number.

Among those who preferred the date given by al-Simnānī, or thereabouts, were the authors of *Akhbār al-Uwwal* and *Rawḍāt al-Jannāt*. Their opinion is supported by the words of Abū Yūsuf himself: 'After languishing for a long time, the people returned to a youth from the people of Medina,' meaning Mālik, as was reported by Ḥāfiẓ Muḥammad ibn Makhlad al-ʿAṭṭār (d.331 AH) in *Mā Rawāhu al-Akābir ʿan Mālik* with his chain of transmission to him. If Abū Yūsuf was not as old as Mālik, or older than him, then he would not have spoken of him in this way. There is a lot of confusion about the dates of birth of the early Muslims, because of how late the books of biography began to be written. Allah knows best. (K)

41 His shaykhs also included Muḥammad ibn Isḥāq (author of *al-Maghāzī*). Al-Muwaffaq al-Khawārizmī narrated in *Manāqib Abī*

He studied jurisprudence under Abū Ḥanīfa, and was

Ḥanīfa, on the authority of Muḥammad ibn Mūsā al-Ḥāsib – Isḥāq ibn Abī Isrā'īl, that Abū Yūsuf used to say:

'I frequented Abū Ḥanīfa to learn from him, but I did not miss out on the chance to hear Hadiths from the narrators. Muḥammad ibn Isḥāq, the author of al-Maghāzī, came to Kufa, and we met with him and asked him to read the Maghāzī to us, which he agreed to do. So I stopped going to see Abū Ḥanīfa for a while, and stayed a few months with Muḥammad ibn Isḥāq until I had heard the whole book from him.

When he finished it, I went back to Abū Ḥanīfa, who said to me, "Ya'qūb, why did you keep away from me?" I said, "It was not that. Muḥammad ibn Isḥāq al-Madīnī came to town, so I studied the Maghāzī with him." He said to me, "Ya'qūb, when you go back to him, ask him who the leader of Ṭālūt was, and who bore the banner of Jālūt." I said, "There is no need for that, Abū Ḥanīfa. By Allah, there is nothing worse than for a man who claims knowledge to be asked which came first, Badr or Uḥud, and not to know the answer!"'

Now there is nothing problematic in this account, for there was nothing wrong with Abū Yūsuf selecting certain things from Muḥammad ibn Isḥāq's knowledge of the Prophetic biography, nor was there anything wrong with Abū Ḥanīfa not having much faith in Muḥammad ibn Isḥāq's knowledge of the Prophetic biography. Abū Ḥanīfa himself studied the Prophetic biography from the likes of al-Sha'bī, whose broad knowledge in that subject was acknowledged by the likes of Ibn 'Umar 🙵. Ibn Isḥāq, on the other hand, had more than one heretical innovation ascribed to him, as Ibn Rajab states in Sharḥ 'Ilal al-Tirmidhī, so it is unobjectionable that Abū Ḥanīfa did not approve of him, just as Mālik did not approve of him. His approach to the science of Prophetic biography was rarely based on sound foundations, and those who approve of Ibn Isḥāq's knowledge of the Prophetic biography do so after deferring to certain well-known conditions. The quotation above does not do an injustice to either side, and there is nothing wrong with its chain of transmission; but what Ibn Khallikān added to the report, when quoting it from al-Mu'āfī al-Nahrawānī al-Jarīrī's

the most eminent of his companions.

---

al-Jalīs al-Ṣāliḥ, was a pure fabrication, whose falsehood is proven by the other narrations concerning the issue.

It was Abū Ḥanīfa who narrated to his companions in his *masānīd* collections of how ʿUmar ﷺ gave more from the treasury to those who fought at Badr than to those who fought at the subsequent battles; and he was ever reciting Allah's words ﴾Allah succoured you at Badr, when you were lowly﴿ [3:123] on the many occasions when he recited the entire Qur'an, by night and by day; now this verse is known to have been revealed at Uḥud, a fact which is known to even beginning students. He also dictated the book *al-Siyar al-Ṣaghīr* to his companions.

This is why al-Awzāʿī rebutted this, and Abū Yūsuf himself was quick to defend Abū Ḥanīfa in his well-known book. How could it be imagined that Abū Yusuf would think Abū Ḥanīfa ignorant of which came first, Badr or Uḥud, even though this is something that everyone knows, except perhaps some schoolchildren? How could it be thought that Abū Yūsuf would be so rude to his teacher, a man whom he is known to have revered on every occasion because of the great part he played in his scholarly training, which included supporting him financially throughout his studies, a great kindness which he would remember for his whole life?

But Ibn Khallikān relished recording anything that criticised the Imam of Imams, from whatever source it came, all the while ignoring anything that criticised his own imam. He was not ashamed to record the fairy-tales of the open drunkard Ḥammād ʿAjrad, nor the story of the 'Prayer of al-Qaffāl,' which no one doubts to be a lie save those whose hearts are utterly sealed.

The author of *al-Jalīs al-Ṣāliḥ* is he who claimed that al-Maʾmūn forced al-Shāfiʿī to drink twenty *raṭl* of wine, which he did, but his mind was not affected by it (*Lisān al-Mīzān*), even though he never met him at all during his caliphate; it is a lie, just like this story. Al-Nahrawānī was not overly diligent when narrating, and his book is a mixture of seriousness and folly, containing unusual stories and laughable eccentricities, even when it comes to things which defame the greatest of imams whilst having the most worthless of chains of transmission. This is the way

Many studied jurisprudence under him. Among those who took narrations from him were Bishr ibn al-Walīd, Ibn Samāʿa, Yaḥyā ibn Maʿīn, ʿAlī ibn al-Jaʿd, Aḥmad ibn Ḥanbal, ʿAmr al-Nāqid, Aḥmad ibn Manīʿ, ʿAlī ibn Muslim al-Ṭūsī, al-Ḥasan ibn Abī Mālik, Hilāl al-Rȧy, Ibrāhīm ibn al-Jarrāḥ, Muʾallā ibn Manṣūr al-Rāzī, Asad ibn al-Furāt and ʿAmr ibn Abī ʿAmr al-Ḥarrānī. The most eminent of his companions was Muḥammad ibn al-Ḥasan.

He was appointed Judge of Baghdad under Mūsā al-Hādī,[42] and then under Hārūn al-Rashīd. He became very renowned, and was the first person to have the title *Qāḍī al-Quḍāh* [Judge of Judges].

Mukram al-Qāḍī reported, on the authority of ʿAbd al-Ṣamad ibn ʿUbayd Allāh – ʿAlī ibn Ḥarmala al-Taymī, that Abū Yūsuf said:

---

it is with the literature of those who are not overly concerned with authenticity. He also narrates from the likes of Muḥammad ibn Abī al-Azhar, Muḥammad ibn al-Ḥasan al-Naqqāsh, Ibn Durayd, Maʿmar ibn Shabīb, al-Ḥasan ibn ʿAlī ibn Zakariyyā al-Baṣrī, ʿAbdallāh ibn Ayyūb ibn Zādān, and others of their ilk whom the scholars of critical enquiry have rejected as liars.

If he narrated from them because he was unaware of their natures, then this is a scandalous embarrassment both for the narrator and for those from whom he narrated; and if he did indeed know their natures, then this is nothing but irreligiousness. This is always the way with those who attempt to harm the great imams with lies: they are their own undoing. We ask Allah for protection. (K)

42 He was actually first appointed judge before this, during the rule of al-Mahdī, as affirmed by Ibn ʿAbd al-Barr in *al-Intiqāʾ* and Muḥammad ibn Khalaf Wakīʿ al-Qāḍī in *Akhbār al-Quḍāh*. (K)

When I first began studying Hadith and jurisprudence, I was very poor. My father[43] came one day when I was with Abū Ḥanīfa and said, 'Son, do not try to march in step with Abū Ḥanīfa, for he always has his bread ready baked, whilst you need to earn a living.' I thought it best to obey my father.

Abū Ḥanīfa asked after me when he remarked on my absence, so I began to attend his gatherings again. When I went, he gave me one hundred dirhams and said to me, 'Keep attending my circles, and when this runs out, let me know.' A short time later, he gave me another hundred, and from thenceforth he continued to support me.

It is also said that his mother was the one who rebuked him, his father having died when he was still in his infancy, and that she gave him over to a bleacher to be his apprentice.

The Praise Scholars Gave Abū Yūsuf

Asad ibn al-Furāt reported that Muḥammad ibn al-Ḥasan said, 'Abū Yūsuf fell ill, and Abū Ḥanīfa went to visit him. When he came out, he said, whilst pointing at the earth: "If this young man dies, he will be the

43 Indeed, it was his father and not his mother, as some versions of the story with weak chains of transmission have it. (K)

most knowledgeable of all those who dwell upon it.'"

ʿAbbās al-Dūrī reported that Aḥmad ibn Ḥanbal said, 'The first time I ever wrote Hadith, I went to Abū Yūsuf, the judge, and transcribed from him. After that, I went to others.' He also said, 'Abū Yūsuf was more to our liking than Abū Ḥanīfa and Muḥammad.'

Ibrāhīm ibn Abī Dāwūd al-Burullusī reported that he heard Yaḥyā ibn Maʿīn say, 'Of all the scholars of reasoned opinion, I never saw any more adept in Hadith, nor anyone with a better memory and sounder narration, than Abū Yūsuf. Abū Ḥanīfa was thoroughly honest, but his narrations of Hadith contained the same things that the narrations other shaykhs contained.' That is, errors.[44]

ʿAbbās al-Dūrī reported that he heard Ibn Maʿīn say, 'Abū Yūsuf was a man of the Hadith and a man of the Sunna.'

44 This explanation offered by al-Dhahabī contradicts the other narrated statements of Ibn Maʿīn, which state that Abū Ḥanīfa 'only narrated what he had memorised, and never narrated what he had not memorised', as well as Abū Ḥanīfa's strictness when it came to narration, as is evident in his statement that 'A man should not report anyone's speech unless he retains it in his memory from the moment he hears it.'

Abū Ḥanīfa did, however, deem it permissible for a *ḥāfiẓ* jurist to relate the meaning of a hadith and not the exact wording, and perhaps in his gatherings he would sometimes relate his understanding of a hadith in brief, or give it without a complete chain when it was already known to those studying in his circle. This is the way it always is in circles of jurisprudence, as opposed to circles of plain narration; it does not amount to any error whatsoever.

Muḥammad ibn Samāʿa reported that Yaḥyā ibn Khālid said: 'Abū Yūsuf came to us, and his knowledge of jurisprudence was so vast as to fill all that lies between the East and the West – and jurisprudence was the least of his talents.'

Bishr ibn al-Walīd reported that he heard Abū Yūsuf say, 'Al-Aʿmash asked me about something, and I answered him. He asked me what I based my opinion on, and I said, "A hadith which you narrated to us." He said, "O Yaʿqūb, I have known this hadith by heart since before your parents met, but I never understood what it meant until now."'

Ibn al-Thaljī reported that he heard ʿAbdallāh ibn Dāwūd al-Khuraybī say, 'Abū Yūsuf had complete mastery of jurisprudence [or he said 'knowledge]: he could utilise it at will.'

ʿAmr ibn Muḥammad al-Nāqid said, 'I do not like to narrate on the authority of any of the men of reasoned opinion, save for Abū Yūsuf; for he was a man of the Sunna.'

Yaḥyā ibn Yaḥyā al-Naysābūrī said, 'I heard Abū Yūsuf say, as he died, "I hereby renounce every legal opinion I ever issued, save those that accord with the Qur'an and Sunna."'[45]

45 This is always the way of those who fear Allah in their religion. It does not mean, though, that he was renouncing every opinion that any Tom, Dick or Harry deems to contradict the Qur'an according to his own interpretation, or is contrary to a hadith he believes to be authentic – for many interpretations are false, and many declarations of authenticity are mistaken, and points of view may differ. These

Ḥanbal reported that he heard Aḥmad ibn Ḥanbal say, 'Abū Yūsuf was fair in his narration.' Al-Fallās said, 'Abū Yūsuf was honest, but he made many mistakes.'[46]

Ibrāhīm ibn Isḥāq al-Zuhrī reported that Bishr al-Marīsī heard Abū Yūsuf say, 'I accompanied Abū Ḥanīfa for seventeen years, and then lived an ordinary worldly life for seven years; and now I think my time has almost come.' Not long after this, he died.

Ibn al-Kās reported that Aḥmad ibn ʿAmmār ibn Abī Mālik heard his father say, 'There was no other companion of Abū Ḥanīfa who could compare to Abū Yūsuf in his knowledge, jurisprudence and understanding. Were it not for him, Abū Ḥanīfa and Ibn Abī Laylā would not have been renowned; for he disseminated their knowledge.'[47]

---

words of Abū Yūsuf are akin to those of al-Shāfiʿī, 'If the hadith is authentic, then that is my school.' This does not mean 'If anyone says the hadith is authentic, I will follow it and renounce what I said before.' Rather, it means: 'If the hadith is authentic according to my criteria of authentication, and if its meaning is clear, then I will follow it.' Otherwise, his school would have been totally confused.

They criticised Abū Muḥammad al-Juwaynī for attempting to author a book collecting every issue for which there was a hadith which in his opinion was authentic and then ascribing this to al-Shāfiʿī based on a literal understanding of this statement. It was clear to the scholars of Hadith that he was declaring inauthentic hadiths to be authentic, and then ascribing the resulting legal interpretation of them to al-Shāfiʿī; and they convinced him to stop doing this. (K)

46 Al-Fallās was biased against the companions of Abū Ḥanīfa. Abū Yūsuf was commended for his memorisation and exactitude by Ibn Ḥibbān and others. (K)

47 This statement is an exaggeration which Abū Yūsuf himself would

Abū Khāzim al-Qāḍī narrated on the authority of Bakr al-ʿAmmī that Hilāl al-Rȧy said, 'Abū Yūsuf memorised exegesis, Prophetic biography and Arab history; jurisprudence was but one of his areas of knowledge.'

Al-Muzanī said, 'Abū Yūsuf followed Hadith more diligently than any other.'

Aḥmad ibn ʿAṭiyya reported that he heard Muḥammad ibn Samāʿa say, 'After he was appointed judge, Abū Yūsuf used to pray two hundred cycles of prayer a day.'

ʿAbbās reported that he heard Yaḥyā ibn Maʿīn say, 'Abū Yūsuf loved the scholars of Hadith, and was inclined towards them.'

ʿAbdallāh ibn ʿAlī al-Madīnī said:

> I heard my father say, 'We used to go to Abū Yūsuf when he came to Basra in the year 180 AH. He would narrate ten hadiths, and then ten reasoned opinions.' I think he also said, 'I find no fault in anything Abū Yūsuf narrated, save for one hadith on the authority of Abū Hishām ibn ʿUrwa concerning the issue of al-ḥajr [juridical

---

not have approved of. Rather, were it not for these two, Abū Yūsuf would not have had his high status at all. He himself said, 'There was no gathering in the world which I loved more to attend than those of Abū Ḥanīfa and Ibn Abī Laylā. I never saw a better jurist than Abū Ḥanīfa, nor a better judge than Ibn Abī Laylā.' This was narrated by al-Ṣaymarī with his chain of transmission. But indeed he was a dutiful student of theirs, and so Allah blessed his knowledge. (K)

interdiction of a spendthrift].[48] He was an honest narrator.'

Some of His Qualities

Al-Ṭaḥāwī narrated, on the authority of Bakkār ibn Qutayba, that Abū al-Walīd al-Ṭayālisī said:

When Abū Yūsuf came to Basra, with al-Rashīd, the scholars of reasoned opinion and the scholars of Hadith all came to his door, each group asking permission to go in to see him first. He looked at them, and did not give leave to either group, saying: 'I am from both groups, and I will not put one ahead of the other. Instead, I will ask a question to both groups, and the ones who give the best answer will be allowed in.'

He then said: 'If a man chews this ring of mine until he crushes it, what right can I demand of him?' The Hadith scholars differed, and he did not approve of what they said. A jurist said, 'He must pay the full value of the ring as it was when it was whole, and he may take the crushed silver, unless the owner of the ring wants to keep it for himself, in which case the one who chewed it does not owe anything.'

48 In fact, this hadith is supported by other narrations; see *al-Talkhīṣ al-Ḥabīr* and *Sunan al-Bayhaqī* . (K)

Abū Yūsuf said, 'The ones who offered this opinion may come in.' I went in with them. The scribe asked him to dictate, and he dictated a hadith on the authority of al-Ḥasan ibn Ṣāliḥ, and said, 'I fear nothing for a man so much as I fear for the one who speaks ill of al-Ḥasan ibn Ṣāliḥ.' I suspected that he meant Shuʿba, so I got up and said, 'I cannot sit in a gathering where Abū Bisṭām [Shuʿba] is maligned,' and then went out.

I returned to my senses, and said to myself, 'This is the greatest judge in the world, and the Caliph's vizier and companion on his pilgrimage, and my anger does not harm him in the least!' I went back and sat down. When the gathering had finished and everyone had gone, he approached me in the manner of a man who was concerned with nothing other than me. 'O Hishām,' he said – for this is how he would address me, since I had been with him in Baghdad – 'by Allah, I meant no ill will towards Abū Bisṭām; as far as I can see, he has a dearer place in my heart than in yours. But I do not think that I have ever seen a man like al-Ḥasan ibn Ṣāliḥ.'

Bakkār said, 'I told this story to Hilāl ibn Yaḥyā [al-Rảy], and he said, "By Allah, I was the one who gave Abū Yūsuf the answer about the ring."'

Ibn al-Thaljī reported that he heard al-Ḥasan ibn Abī Mālik say:

I heard Abū Yūsuf say, 'Were I able to divide all the knowledge in my heart amongst you all, I would do it.'

I also heard him say: 'I once fell so ill that I forgot everything I had ever memorised, even the Qur'an! But I did not forget jurisprudence, because my knowledge of everything apart from jurisprudence was obtained by memorisation, whilst my knowledge of jurisprudence was obtained by guidance. If a man is away from his hometown for a long while, and then returns, will he forget the way to his house?'

Hilāl al-Rảy reported that he heard Abū Yūsuf say, 'Rudeness to rulers brings ignominy; rudeness to judges brings poverty.' He also reported that he heard him say about written contracts and the like, 'One needs at least ten witnesses, for two will die, two will be absent, two will not fulfil their promise, two will be firm, and two will be false.'

Muḥammad ibn Shujāʿ reported that he heard al-Ḥasan ibn Abī Mālik say:

I heard Abū Yūsuf say, 'The Qur'an is the Speech of Allah, and anyone who asks how or why, and stirs up debates and disputes, should be imprisoned and beaten severely.'

I also heard him say, 'No success will come to those who are bewitched by the sweetness of speculative theology.'

I also heard him say, 'One should not pray behind anyone who says that the Qur'an is created.'

ʿAlī ibn al-Jaʿd reported that he heard Abū Yūsuf say, 'Whoever claims to have faith like the faith of Jibrīl is a heretic.'

Aḥmad ibn Abī ʿImrān al-Faqīh reported that Faraj, the freedman of Abū Yūsuf, said, 'I saw my master Abū Yūsuf raising his hands when he made the *qunūt* supplication in the *witr* prayer.' This is if Faraj was trustworthy.[49]

Abū Khāzim al-Qāḍī narrated, on the authority of al-Ḥasan ibn Mūsā, the Judge of Hamadhān, that Bishr ibn al-Walīd said:

When Abū Yūsuf mentioned Muḥammad ibn al-Ḥasan, he would say, 'What a sword he is, save that he is rusty and needs polishing.'

When he mentioned al-Ḥasan ibn Ziyād, he would say, 'For me, he is like an apothecary: when a man asks for something to loosen his bowels, he gives him something to tighten them!'

When he mentioned Bishr, he would say, 'He is like a darner's needle: sharp, but breaks easily.'

When he mentioned al-Ḥasan ibn Abī Mālik, he

49 Ibn Abī al-ʿAwwām says, 'Ibn Abī ʿImrān told us that no one conveyed this to him from Abū Yūsuf except Faraj, and he was trustworthy.' So it might be 'Faraj was trustworthy' [rather than 'if Faraj was trustworthy']. (W)
The same is found in *al-Jawāhir al-Muḍiyya*. (K)

would say, 'He is like a camel bearing a load on a rainy day: slipping to and fro but not falling.'

Al-Ṭaḥāwī narrated, on the authority of Abū ʿImrān, who heard it from Muḥammad ibn Samāʿa, that Abū Yūsuf said, 'Rabīʿa ibn Abī ʿAbd al-Raḥmān[50] came to town, so I went to see him and said, "What do you say about a slave owned jointly by two men, one of whom frees him?" He said, "The manumission is invalid." I said, "If what you say is true, then if the other frees him as well, that would also be invalid! And if it is not valid for his owners to free him, then who else is going to free him?"'

Abū Bakr al-Khaṣṣāf reported, on the authority of his father, that al-Ḥasan ibn Ziyād said:

> One day we were at Abū Yūsuf's door when he approached from the direction of al-Rashīd's residence, smiling. He said:
>
> 'Something has arisen in the house of the Commander of the Faithful. A judge in Armenia was presented with the case of two slave-girls and two jars: they went to draw water and then put the jugs down so they could relieve themselves, but one jar fell onto the other and they both broke. They took their case to the judge, each one claiming that it was the jar of the other which fell onto her jar and broke it.

50 He was the shaykh of Mālik in jurisprudence, but found it difficult to debate Abū Yūsuf on issues, which is why Mālik declined to debate him in al-Rashīd's court, according to Ibn ʿAsākir in *Kashf al-Mughaṭṭā*. (K)

'The judge began to examine each one, but could not work out who was the plaintiff and who the defendant. He told his assistant to delay their case, but they began to yell and kick up a fuss. Finally he told his assistant to go out and buy them both jugs, to please them both.

'That night, he asked a close friend of his what the people were saying about him. He told him that they were saying, "The judge is not even skilled enough to judge a matter of two jars, and had to pay them both off!" He said, "Glory be to Allah! Are they not happy for me to judge on those matters that I do well, and pay out for those matters that I do not do well?"'

Abū Yūsuf continued, 'I said, "O Commander of the Faithful, this is an intelligent man! Increase his budget for pay-outs by a thousand dirhams a month."'

I said to Abū Yūsuf, 'How should the case have been settled?' He replied, 'If they put the jugs down in a [public] privy belonging to the Muslims, then they both had the right to put their jugs there and neither one of them wronged the other disproportionately, so they each owe the other the value of her jug. If one of them was in a privy and the other was not, then the one who was not in the privy wronged the other.'

Bishr ibn al-Walīd reported that he heard Abū Yūsuf say, 'The one who seeks wealth through alchemy will end up bankrupt; the one who seeks knowledge through speculative theology will end up astray; and the one who seeks out rare hadiths will end up a liar.'

Muḥammad ibn Saʿd reported that Abū Sulaymān al-Jūzajānī told him he heard Abū Yūsuf say, 'I went to see al-Rashīd, and found him turning two pearls over in his hand. "O Yaʿqūb," he said, "have you ever seen anything finer than these?" I said, "Yes." He said, "And what was it?" I said, "The vessel which contains them." He threw them to me, and said, "Do as you please with them." I took them, and went my way.'

Al-Ṭaḥāwī reported, on the authority of Ibn Abī ʿImrān – Muḥammad ibn Shujāʿ – al-Ḥasan ibn Abī Mālik, that Abū Yūsuf said during his final illness:

> By Allah, I have never committed adultery, nor judged unjustly. I do not fear for any action of mine save one: I used to take people's cases and read them to al-Rashīd, and then rule on them in his presence. Once, I took the case of a Christian who laid claim to an estate which was in al-Rashīd's possession, and which he claimed al-Rashīd had forcibly seized from him. I summoned the Christian and read his case to al-Rashīd, who said, 'That estate is ours; we inherited it from al-Manṣūr.' I said to the Christian, 'You heard what he said; do you have any proof to offer?' He said, 'No, but have him swear to it.' I said, 'Will you swear, O Commander of the Faithful?' He said, 'Yes,' and he swore to it. The Christian then left. So I fear that I did not hold

a proper tribunal between the Christian and the Commander of the Faithful.

ʿAlī ibn al-Jaʿd reported that he heard a man ask Abū Yūsuf, 'Some people say that you consider valid the testimony of a man who holds that Allah does not know things until they happen. Is this true?' He replied, 'Woe betide you! If he repents, then yes; otherwise, I deem he should be executed.'

Bishr ibn al-Walīd reported that he heard Abū Yūsuf say during his final illness, 'O Allah, You know that I never engaged in unlawful sexual intercourse, nor ever knowingly consumed a single unlawfully earned dirham!'

Ibn al-Kås reported, on the authority of Abū ʿAmr al-Qazwīnī, that al-Qāsim ibn al-Ḥakam reported that he heard Abū Yūsuf say before his death, 'Would that I could die with the same level of jurisprudential knowledge I once had! By Allah, since I became a judge I never deliberately judged unjustly, nor was I ever biased for one appellant against another, whether a ruler or a peddler.'

Al-Ṭaḥāwī reported, on the authority of Aḥmad ibn Abī ʿImrān, who heard it from Dāwūd ibn Wahb, that ʿAbd al-Raḥmān al-Qawwās (of whom it was said that no one in Baghdad was superior to him) said:

> Maʿrūf al-Karkhī said to me, 'When Abū Yūsuf dies, let me know.' I went off, and found myself walking beside the funeral procession of none other

than Abū Yūsuf. I went along with it, thinking that if I went back to Maʿrūf, I would miss the funeral, and he would not make it in time anyway.

So afterwards, I went to him and said, 'Had I come back to you, you would not have made it in time.' He became downcast. I asked him why, and he said, 'Last night, I had a dream of being admitted into Paradise, where I saw a palace. I asked whose it was, and the answer came, "It belongs to Yaʿqūb [Abū Yūsuf] al-Qāḍī." I said, "What did he do to earn it?" The answer came, "He taught knowledge to others, and people said many bad things about him."'

ʿAbdallāh ibn Aḥmad ibn Ḥanbal reported that he heard his father say, 'Abū Yūsuf, may Allah may mercy on him, had a speech impediment.[51] When he wanted to say *Muṭarrif ibn Ṭarīf al-Ḥārithī*, he would say *Muṭayyif ibn Ṭayīf al-Ḥāyithī*.'

Abū Ḥassān al-Ziyādī said, 'Abū Yūsuf was al-Rashīd's judge, and appointed as his successor his son Yūsuf, who used to judge alongside him. When Abū Yūsuf died, al-Rashīd retained his son as judge, until Yūsuf died.'

Al-Ḥasan ibn Ḥammād Sajjāda reported that he heard Yūsuf ibn Abī Yūsuf say, 'I was appointed judge, as was my father before me. All together, we served

51 It is known that al-Rashīd could not stand this sort of speech impediment, so the facts of the matter indicate that this report is inauthentic, especially considering that the person who narrated it from ʿAbdallāh was an errant anthropomorphist. (K)

as judge for thirty years, not worrying about judging between a grandfather and a brother.'

Ibn ʿAdī said of Abū Yūsuf, 'There is no fault in him [as a narrator].' Abū Ḥātim al-Rāzī said, 'His hadiths may be written.'[52] Abū ʿAbdallāh al-Bukhārī said, 'They have rejected him.'[53] Abū Ḥafṣ al-Fallās said, 'He was honest, but made many errors.'

I say that there are many reports of the nobility, generosity, chivalry, great distinction and utmost respectability in knowledge and virtue of the *Qāḍī al-Quḍāh*, Abū Yūsuf (may Allah have mercy on him and be well pleased with him). There are also some reports which criticise him, some of which are inauthentic,

52 Ibn al-Jawzī (in *Akhbār al-Ḥuffāẓ*) named him as one of the hundred most notable Hadith scholars of this community in terms of sheer power of memory; he would dictate around sixty hadiths with their full chains to his students in a single session. This was also affirmed by Ibn ʿAbd al-Barr before him, and Ibn Ḥibbān before him, and Ibn Jarīr before him, who said in *Dhayl al-Madhīl*, 'He was known for memorising Hadiths, and would sit with a Hadith scholar and memorise fifty or sixty Hadiths [in a single session], and then go and dictate them to the people. He memorised many Hadiths.' Aḥmad ibn Kāmil al-Shajarī said in *Tārīkh al-Quḍāh*, 'Yaḥyā ibn Maʿīn, Aḥmad ibn Ḥanbal and ʿAlī ibn al-Madīnī were all agreed that he was a trusted narrator.' (K)

53 Ibn Abī Ḥātim says in *al-Jarḥ wal-Taʿdīl* of al-Bukhārī, 'Abū Zurʿa and Abū Ḥātim rejected him.' Now this is a serious thing to be said about the greatest of all Hadith scholars! Likewise, what al-Bukhārī said about Abū Yūsuf, the great and diligent imam, *mujtahid* and *ḥāfiẓ*, was outside the bounds of fairness. Perhaps what Ibn Abī Ḥātim said about al-Bukhārī was Allah's way of avenging Abū Yūsuf! Otherwise, neither one of them was a rejected narrator. (K)

which have been narrated by al-ʿUqaylī,[54] Ibn Thābit[55] (in *Tārīkh Baghdād*) and others.

ʿAlī ibn Salama al-Labaqī reported that he heard

54 He was a vicious anthropomorphist, who did not fail to slake his lust for attacking Abū Ḥanīfa and every one of his companions. He did not mention a single virtue of any of them, and blackened the biographies he wrote for them with clear evidence of the rancour he harboured towards the people of truth. He was thoroughly refuted by one of his own narrators, Ibn al-Dakhīl al-Ṣaydalānī, in a separate volume he authored on the virtues of Abū Ḥanīfa, which he transmitted to al-Ḥakam ibn al-Mudhir, who in turn transmitted it to his companion Ibn ʿAbd al-Barr, who then included most of it in *al-Intiqāʾ fī Akhbār al-Aʾimma al-Thalātha al-Fuqahāʾ*, which was more than ample. Al-Dhahabī says in *al-Mīzān* in the entry for ʿAlī ibn al-Madīnī, after mentioning some men whom this same ʿUqaylī attacked: 'Were the hadiths which these men narrated to be abandoned, the door would be closed upon us, and all scholarship and tradition would perish, and heretics would become ascendant, and the Antichrist himself would come forth! Do you not have a mind, ʿUqaylī? Do you even know of whom you speak? It is as if you do not know that every one of these men is many times more reliable than you are!' (K)

55 Ibn Thābit is al-Khaṭīb al-Baghdādī, author of *Tārīkh Baghdād*. He harmed himself by what he did, as I have already unveiled in *Taʾnīb al-Khaṭīb*. He related some bizarre fabrications concerning the members of our school, with chains of transmission containing narrators even he considered to be liars. One place he did this was in his entry for Abū Yūsuf, including a tale in which he supposedly employed a legal ruse to make a slave-girl lawful for al-Rashīd in a way which any religious person would reject, a tale which contained obvious exaggerations. Yet the chain of transmission he offered for this story contained Muḥammad ibn Abī al-Azhar, of whom he said elsewhere, 'He was a liar who told ugly lies.' Woe betide him who supports a story with a man he deems to be 'a liar who tells ugly lies,' in order to attack a great imam like Abū Yūsuf! (K)

Yaḥyā ibn Yaḥyā say, 'I went to visit Abū Yūsuf in Jurjān when he was ill. He said, "I testify that I have renounced every legal opinion I gave the people, save those which are backed by the Qur'an and the consensus of the Muslims."'[56]

Bishr ibn al-Walīd said, 'Abū Yūsuf (may Allah have mercy on him) died on Thursday on the fifth of Rabīʿ al-Awwal in the year 182 AH.' Others say that it was in the month of Rabīʿ al-Ākhir. He died in Baghdad, at the age of sixty-nine.[57]

56 This is a fabrication, and one need look no further for the evidence of this than the tale itself. Firstly, his method was not to restrict evidence to the Qur'an and consensus; rather, he followed the Sunna in its different types, and then analogy as well. Secondly, the people of scholarship and history agree that he died in Baghdad, not Jurjān. Thirdly, some of his companions narrated legal opinions which he issued on his deathbed, and they were not restricted to the Qur'an and consensus. Fourthly, the chain of transmission of this story contains Aḥmad ibn Ḥafṣ al-Jurjānī, who was a known fabricator. Moreover, there is not a single scholar of Islam who issues legal opinions without knowing what the Qur'an and consensus say on the matter, nor any who issues opinions which contradict them knowingly, such that a renunciation such as this could be imagined.
The wording of al-Khaṭīb differs from this one, even though he too narrated it through Aḥmad ibn Ḥafṣ on the authority of al-Labaqī. The wording of Yaḥyā ibn Yaḥyā as narrated by al-Khaṭīb is: 'I heard Abū Yūsuf al-Qāḍī say when he died, "I hereby renounce every legal opinion I ever issued, save for those which accord with the Book of Allah and the Sunna of the Messenger of Allah ﷺ."'
Now, is there any jurist who does not renounce his opinion – at any time in his life – if he realises that it does not accord with the Qur'an or the Sunna because of some error on his part? (K)
57 This is according to the most widely-accepted opinion of his date

Yaʿqūb ibn Shayba reported that he heard Shujāʿ ibn Makhlad say, 'We attended the funeral of Abū Yūsuf, and ʿAbbād ibn al-ʿAwwām said, "All the Muslims should console one another for the death of Abū Yūsuf."'

SOME HADITHS HE NARRATED

We have it on the authority of Aḥmad ibn Isḥāq al-Abraqūhī (in the year 695 AH) – al-Mubārak ibn Abī al-Jūd – Aḥmad ibn al-Ṭallāya – Abū al-Qāsim al-Anmāṭī – Abū Ṭāhir al-Mukhalliṣ – Abū Ḥāmid al-Ḥaḍramī – Isḥāq ibn Abī Isrāʾīl – **Abū Yūsuf** – Abū Ḥanīfa – ʿAlqama ibn Marthad – Sulaymān ibn Burayda that his father [Burayda] said, 'The family of Māʿiz asked the Messenger of Allah ﷺ for permission to bury him and pray his funeral prayer, and he gave them permission to do so.'

We have it on the authority of ʿAbd al-ʿAzīẓ ibn Hibat Allāh al-ʿUqaylī al-Ḥanafī – Yūsuf ibn Khalīl – ʿAbd al-Khāliq ibn al-Ṣābūnī and ʿAbd al-Raḥmān ibn Naṣr Allāh al-Bayyiʿ, both on the authority of Qarātikīn ibn Asʿad – Abū Muḥammad al-Jawharī – al-Qāḍī Abū Bakr al-Abharī – Abū ʿArūba al-Ḥarrānī – his grandfather ʿAmr ibn Abī ʿAmr – **Abū**

---

of birth. According to the opinion of Abū al-Qāsim al-Simnānī and Ibn Faḍl Allāh al-ʿUmari, he was eighty-nine years old when he died. Allah knows best. (K)

Yūsuf Ya'qūb ibn Ibrāhīm – 'Ubayd Allāh ibn 'Umar – Nāfi', that Ibn 'Umar said, 'Even if I only had a double handful of water, I would use it to perform the greater ablution.'

We also have it, with the same chain of transmission up to **Abū Yūsuf** – Abū Ḥanīfa – 'Aṭā' ibn Abī Rabāh, that Ibn 'Abbās said, 'Kissing does not nullify ablution.'

We have it, on the authority of Abū al-Ghanā'im ibn 'Allān, al-Mu'ammal ibn Muḥammad and Yūsuf ibn Ya'qūb, all of them on the authority of Zayd ibn al-Ḥasan al-Muqri' – 'Abd al-Raḥmān ibn Ruzayq al-Shaybānī – Aḥmad ibn 'Alī al-Ḥāfiẓ – Abū 'Umar ibn Mahdī – Muḥammad ibn Makhlad – 'Abdūs ibn Bishr al-Rāzī – Abū Yūsuf al-Qāḍī – Abū Ḥanīfa – Nāfi', that Ibn 'Umar said, 'The Messenger of Allah ﷺ said, **"On Friday, one should perform the greater ablution."'**

We have it, on the authority of Ismā'īl ibn 'Abd al-Raḥmān – Abū al-Qāsim ibn Ṣaṣrā – 'Alī ibn Surūr al-Khashshāb – al-Ḥasan ibn Aḥmad ibn Muḥammad ibn Abī al-Ḥadīd (in the year 480 AH) – al-Musaddad ibn 'Alī al-Umlūkī – Ismā'īl ibn al-Qāsim al-Ḥalabī (in Homs, 370 AH) – Yaḥyā ibn 'Alī ibn Hāshim al-Kindī – his maternal grandfather Muḥammad ibn Ibrāhīm ibn Abī Sukayna al-Ḥalabī – **Abū Yūsuf** – Ismā'īl ibn Abī Khālid – Qays, that Ibn Mas'ūd said, 'The Messenger of Allah ﷺ said, **"There should be no envy, save for two: a man to whom Allah gives wealth and guides him to spend it in the way of the truth, and a man to whom**

Allah gives knowledge which he then teaches and applies.'"

Praise be to Allah, Lord of the Worlds

THREE

IMAM MUḤAMMAD IBN AL-ḤASAN AL-SHAYBĀNĪ

IN THE Name of Allah, the Compassionate, the Merciful. Praise be to Allah, Lord of the Worlds. May Allah bless our master Muḥammad and all his Family and Companions.

This is a biography of Imam Muḥammad ibn al-Ḥasan al-Shaybānī, whose full name was Muḥammad ibn al-Ḥasan ibn Farqad al-Shaybānī Mawlāhum; or according to some: Muḥammad ibn al-Ḥasan ibn ʿUbayd Allāh ibn Marwān.[58] His father was from Ḥarastā, a well-known town near Damascus, and moved to Iraq towards the end of the Umayyad era. Muḥammad was born to him in Wāsiṭ in the year 302 AH. He then took him to Kufa, where he grew up. He studied a little under Abū Ḥanīfa, and then kept the company of Abū Yūsuf until he mastered jurisprudence.

58 This is unreliable, which is why it is introduced with a vague expression [ʻaccording to some']. All they differed over was whether he was affiliated with the Shaybān tribe by blood, or not. ʻAbd al-Qahhār al-Baghdādī said, 'He was a Shaybānī by blood.' (K)

He also studied under Misʿar ibn Kidām, Mālik ibn Mighwal, ʿUmar ibn Dharr al-Hamdānī, Sufyān al-Thawrī, al-Awzāʿī and Mālik ibn Anas; he spent a fair amount of time with Mālik. After Abū Yūsuf's passing, he became the leader of the jurists of Iraq. Many imams studied under him.[59]

He authored several works, and was one of the most intelligent scholars of his time. He was given the post of *Qāḍī al-Quḍāh* under al-Rashīd, and attained the highest level of prestige and renown.

He took narrations from al-Shāfiʿī, Abū ʿUbayd al-Qāsim ibn Sallām, Hishām ibn ʿUbayd Allāh al-Rāzī, ʿAlī ibn Muslim al-Ṭūsī, ʿAmr ibn Abī ʿAmr, Yaḥyā ibn Maʿīn, Muḥammad ibn Samāʿa, Yaḥyā ibn Ṣāliḥ al-Wuḥāẓī and others.

Muḥammad ibn Saʿd said, 'His origins were in Arabia. His father lived for a time in Syria, and then moved to Wāsiṭ, where Muḥammad was born. He studied with many, and tried his hand at reasoned opinion and mastered it. He settled in Baghdad, and many people frequented him and studied under him.'

Aḥmad ibn ʿAṭiyya reported that he heard ʿUbayd say, 'I never saw anyone with greater knowledge of the Book of Allah than Muḥammad ibn al-Ḥasan.'

Al-Rabīʿ ibn Sulaymān reported that he heard al-Shāfiʿī say, 'Muḥammad ibn al-Ḥasan was so eloquent that if I wished to say that the Qur'an was revealed in his language, I could.'

59 Such as al-Shāfiʿī, Abū ʿUbayd and Asad ibn al-Furāt, may Allah have mercy on them. (K)

Abū Bakr ibn al-Mundhir reported, on the authority of al-Muzanī, that al-Shāfiʿī said, 'I never saw a corpulent man with a lighter spirit than Muḥammad ibn al-Ḥasan, nor did I ever see anyone more eloquent than him. When I saw him recite, it was as though the Qur'an had been revealed in his language.'

Ismāʿīl ibn Ḥammād ibn Abī Ḥanīfa reported that Muḥammad ibn al-Ḥasan said, 'I heard that Dāwūd al-Ṭāʾī used to ask about me and about my health, and say, "If he lives, greatness awaits him."'

Idrīs ibn Yūsuf al-Qarāṭīsī reported that he heard al-Shāfiʿī say, 'I never saw anyone with greater knowledge of the Qur'an than Muḥammad. It was as though it had been revealed to him.'

Al-Ṭaḥāwī reported, on the authority of Aḥmad ibn Abī Dāwūd al-Makkī, who heard it from Ḥarmala ibn Yaḥyā, that al-Shāfiʿī said, 'I never saw anyone who spoke in such a way that it seemed as if the Qur'an had been revealed in his language, save for Muḥammad ibn al-Ḥasan. I wrote enough of his teachings to load my camel.'

Muḥammad ibn Ismāʿīl al-Raqqī reported, on the authority of al-Rabīʿ, that al-Shāfiʿī said, 'I filled enough books with Muḥammad ibn al-Ḥasan's teachings to load my camel. Everyone I ever debated showed his frustration in his face, except Muḥammad ibn al-Ḥasan.'

Ibn Abī Ḥātim reported, on the authority of al-Rabīʿ, that al-Shāfiʿī said, 'I took enough of Muḥammad ibn al-Ḥasan's teachings to load my camel; all they contained was what I heard from him.'

Aḥmad ibn Abī Surayj al-Rāzī reported that he heard al-Shāfiʿī say, 'I spent sixty dirhams on the books of Muḥammad ibn al-Ḥasan, and then reflected on them; and beside every single issue, I wrote a hadith.'

Al-Shāfiʿī is also reported to have said, 'I never debated a corpulent man more intelligent than Muḥammad ibn al-Ḥasan. I debated him once, and his veins began to throb, and his buttons popped open.'

ʿAbbās ibn Muḥammad reported that Ibn Maʿīn said, 'I wrote down *al-Jāmiʿ al-Ṣaghīr* from Muḥammad ibn al-Ḥasan's dictation.'

Abū Khāzim al-Qāḍī narrated, on the authority of Bakr al-ʿAmmī, that Muḥammad ibn Samāʿa said, 'Muḥammad ibn al-Ḥasan's heart would become so absorbed in thinking about an issue of jurisprudence that a man might greet him, call him "Muḥammad," and then add something to the greeting, and he would reply to him with the exact same words, calling him by his own name as though it were part of the greeting.'

Al-Ṭaḥāwī reported that Muḥammad ibn Shādhān heard al-Akhfash al-Naḥwī say, 'Nothing ever matched something so perfectly as Muḥammad ibn al-Ḥasan's book on oaths, for it exactly matched what all the scholars said.'

Muḥammad ibn Samāʿa said that Muḥammad ibn al-Ḥasan often embodied the following verse:

> They are envied,[60] but the worst of men

60 Al-Muwaffaq has: 'They envy me,' and Ibn Abī al-ʿAwwām has it

Is he who lives without ever being envied.

Yūnus ibn ʿAbd al-Aʿlā reported that he heard al-Shāfiʿī say:

> I said to Muḥammad ibn al-Ḥasan, 'You say, "Your companion [Mālik] hardly ever spoke, and my companion [Abū Ḥanīfa] was hardly ever silent."[61] I ask you by Allah: Do you know that my companion was knowledgeable of the Book of Allah?' He said yes. I said, 'And was he knowledgeable of the hadiths of the Messenger of Allah ﷺ?' He said yes. I said, 'And was he intelligent?' He said yes.
>
> I said, 'Now, was your companion ignorant of the Book of Allah?' He said yes. 'And of what has been narrated from the Messenger of Allah?' He said yes.[62] I said, 'And was he intelligent?' He said yes.

---

as it is here. (K)

61 Al-Harawī's narration in *Dhamm al-Kalām* has: 'I saw Mālik and asked him about some things, but he did not have the right to give a single opinion...'

62 This was added by al-Khaṭīb, and al-Dhahabī did not scrutinise it and simply copied what al-Khaṭīb had written. The proof of this is that the reality of the matter contradicts it: if Muḥammad ibn al-Ḥasan had really viewed Abū Ḥanīfa as ignorant, Muḥammad would not have spent his life studying, codifying and disseminating his legal methodology to the horizons.

Now al-Khaṭīb relates this story on the authority of Yūnus ibn ʿAbd al-Aʿlā, from whom Ibn ʿAbd al-Barr also related it via Muḥammad ibn al-Rabīʿ and Muḥammad ibn Sufyān in *al-Intiqāʾ* with the following

I said, 'Your companion has three qualities which any would-be judge must have.' (Or he [Yūnus] said something like this.)

---

wording: 'Al-Shāfiʿ said to me, "I spoke with Muḥammad ibn al-Ḥasan one day, and we debated and differed, until I saw that his veins were throbbing and his buttons were popping open. One of the things I said to him on that day was, 'We ask you by Allah, do you know that our companion', meaning Mālik, 'was knowledgeable of the Book of Allah?' He said yes. I said, 'And knowledgeable of the differences of opinion of the Messenger of Allah's ﷺ Companions?' He said yes."'

This is how the narration of Ibn ʿAbd al-Barr ends. What relation does this bear to the version that al-Khaṭīb relates? Yet they are both given on the authority of Yūnus ibn ʿAbd al-Aʿlā. The narration of Ibn ʿAbd al-Barr contains no description of Abū Ḥanīfa as being ignorant of the Qur'an and Sunna; it was a ruse of al-Khaṭīb himself to add this description.

Then al-Khaṭīb ends his narration with the words 'Or he said something like this,' so that if his addition were exposed, he could say, 'I never claimed that this is exactly what Yūnus said; I only said he said something like this.' Look at this blatant treachery on the part of al-Khaṭīb!

Now there is great confusion about this story because of the disparate ways in which it has been narrated by different sources. Examine the narration of Ibn ʿAbd al-Barr in *al-Intiqā'*, Abū Isḥāq al-Shīrāzī in *Ṭabaqāṭ al-Fuqahā'*, the anthropomorphist al-Harawī in *Dhamm al-Kalām*, Ibn al-Jawzī in *Manāqib Aḥmad* and al-Khaṭīb (as given here), and you will find that they are extremely confused in wording and meaning. I examined this at greater length in *Ta'nīb al-Khaṭīb*.

What is important is that if Muḥammad ibn al-Ḥasan regarded Abū Ḥanīfa in the way that al-Khaṭīb wishes to depict, then he would not have devoted his life to the legal methodology of Abū Ḥanīfa, nor would he have followed the methodology he did in his book *al-Ḥujja ʿalā Ahl al-Madīna*. (K)

Ibrāhīm ibn Abī Dāwūd al-Burullusī reported that he heard Yaḥyā ibn Ṣāliḥ al-Wuḥāẓī say:

> I went on the pilgrimage with Muḥammad ibn al-Ḥasan, and said to him, 'Narrate your book on jurisprudence to me.' He said, 'I do not have the energy to do it.' I said, 'Then let me read it to you.' He said, 'Which do you suppose would be easier for me: to read it to you, or for you to read it to me?' I said, 'For me to read it to you.' He said, 'No, it would be easier for me to read it to you, since I would then only use my eyes and my tongue; yet if you read it to me, then I would have to use my eyes, my mind and my ears.'

Sulaymān ibn Shuʿayb al-Kaysānī reported that his father heard Muḥammad ibn al-Ḥasan say:

> If there is a difference of opinion about something, and one jurist declares it forbidden while another declares it permitted, both of them being qualified for ijtihād, then there is only one right answer in Allah's sight: permitted, or forbidden. Nothing is both permitted and forbidden in His sight. As for those who say, 'One jurist said that this is permitted, and another that it is forbidden, and they are both right in Allah's sight,' it is something that should never be said. Rather, it should be said that there is only one right answer in Allah's sight, and that the people fulfilled their duty when they engaged

in *ijtihād*, and they did the best they could. This is the opinion of Abū Ḥanīfa, Abū Yūsuf, and us.

Aḥmad ibn Abī ʿImrān reported that he heard Muḥammad ibn Shujāʿ say, despite his divergence from the positions of Muḥammad ibn al-Ḥasan: 'Never has there been produced in Islam a book like Muḥammad ibn al-Ḥasan's *al-Jāmiʿ al-Kabīr.*'

Muḥammad ibn ʿAbdallāh ibn ʿAbd al-Ḥakam and others report on the authority of al-Shāfiʿī that Muḥammad ibn al-Ḥasan said, 'I stayed by Mālik's door for three years, and heard over seven hundred hadiths word-for-word from him.' Al-Shāfiʿī added:

> When Muḥammad ibn al-Ḥasan narrated from Mālik, his house would fill up with people so that they were crammed in. When he narrated from anyone other than Mālik, only a few people would attend. He would say, 'I do not know anyone who treats his own companions worse than you do! If I narrate to you [from Mālik, you fill up the place, but if I narrate to you][63] from your own companions, you only come reluctantly.'[64]

63 The addition between brackets is from Ibn Abī al-ʿAwwām. (W)

64 Their excuse for this was that the narrators of Iraq were so numerous that no one feared that their hadiths would be lost, unlike the hadiths of Mālik in Iraq after his death, which were known only to the likes of Imam Muḥammad ibn al-Ḥasan. So for them to be more eager to hear Mālik's hadiths was not something for which they could be blamed. (K)

Al-Ṭaḥāwī reported, on the authority of Aḥmad ibn Abī ʿImrān, that Muḥammad ibn Samāʿa heard Muḥammad ibn al-Ḥasan say, 'This book' – meaning *al-Ḥiyal* – 'is not one of our books; it is a forgery.' Ibn Abī ʿImrān added, 'It was authored by Ismāʿīl ibn Ḥammād ibn Abī Ḥanīfa.'[65]

Al-Ṭaḥāwī reported on the authority of Yūnus ibn ʿAbd al-Aʿlā that al-Shāfiʿī said: 'When Muḥammad ibn al-Ḥasan sat down to debate on jurisprudence, he would appoint an arbitrator between himself and whomever he debated, who would determine who had won and lost each issue. It is said that this man was ʿĪsā ibn Marwān.'

Mūsā ibn Nuṣayr reported that Hishām ibn ʿUbayd Allāh al-Rāzī said:

> We set out from Medina [to Mecca] with Muḥammad ibn al-Ḥasan. When we reached Dhul-Ḥalīfa, we dismounted with him; it was shortly before midday. He went off somewhere, I presume to make ablutions, and then put on a loincloth and robe. The time for the midday prayer arrived, so he walked off and we followed, until he came to the mosque, where he led us in two cycles of

65 Perhaps Ismāʿīl had a book about legal solutions and stratagems which we have not seen; but the book which contains the most devious of legal stratagems [*ḥiyal*] was narrated by the liar, son of the liar, son of the liar, Muḥammad ibn al-Ḥusayn ibn Ḥumayd, from Muḥammad ibn Bishr al-Raqqī, from Khalaf ibn Bayyan: a narration from two unknown men in a row! We ask Allah for security. (K)

prayer. Then he recited the talibiya and we joined him in it. He then made the intention to begin a simultaneous greater and lesser pilgrimage.

He then went to his mount, reciting the talbiya all the while. He had led his sacrificial offering all the way from Medina. Once he had entered the consecrated state and recited the talbiya, he instructed the camel-herder to make the sacrificial mark on his offering, which was fat, with a knife. Muḥammad looked on as he marked it on the left side above the shoulder at the base of the hump, so that blood could be seen flowing from it.

Ibrāhīm al-Ḥarbī said, 'I asked Aḥmad ibn Ḥanbal, "Where do you get your positions on these intricate matters?" He replied, "From the books of Muḥammad ibn al-Ḥasan."'

Abū ʿArūba reported, on the authority of ʿAmr ibn Abī ʿAmr, that Muḥammad ibn al-Ḥasan said, 'My father left me thirty thousand dirhams. I spent fifteen thousand on grammar and poetry, and the other fifteen thousand on Hadith and jurisprudence.'

Ibn Samāʿa reported that Muḥammad ibn al-Ḥasan said to his family, 'Do not ask me for any worldly need and thereby distract my heart. Take what you need from my clerk, for that is less distracting for my heart and causes me less worry.'[66]

66 One nice story about this is related by al-Khaṭīb in *al-ʿUzla*, although its chain of transmission is not authentic. He relates that al-Ḥusayn ibn al-Faqīh heard that when Muḥammad ibn al-Ḥasan (Allah have

Ibn Kaʾs al-Nakhaʿī reported, on the authority of Aḥmad ibn Ḥammād [ibn] Sufyān, that al-Rabīʿ ibn Sulaymān heard al-Shāfiʿī say, 'I never saw anyone more intelligent, more skilled in jurisprudence, more ascetic, more scrupulous, or finer in speech and narration than Muḥammad ibn al-Ḥasan.' I say that no one but Aḥmad ibn Ḥammād relates this from al-Rabīʿ, and it is dubious.[67]

---

mercy on him) began to author *al-Jamiʿ al-Kabīr*, he secluded himself in a cellar and instructed his family to pay attention to his mealtimes and ablution times and bring him what he needed for them, to cut his hair when it grew too long, to clean his clothes when they grew dirty, and not to disturb him with anything. He put a clerk in charge of his money and gave him total control of it, and then began writing the book. He was so absorbed with it that he did not notice that a man had come in, until he went and stood right in front of him. He did not recognise him, and asked who he was. The man replied, 'I am the owner of this house!' He asked how this could be. The man said, 'Your clerk sold it to me!' Now because he had given the clerk full control of his possessions, he was forced to move house. (K)

67 Al-Dhahabī has no basis for saying this, because Ibn Kās was a trusted narrator, and al-Khaṭīb himself, despite his obstinacy, declared Aḥmad ibn Ḥammād ibn Sufyān to be trustworthy. Al-Dāraquṭnī said of him, 'There is no fault in him.' There is no record of him being declared weak. The report itself is backed up by several others which are similar. Al-Dhahabī's words are not in line with the scholarly rules of critical examination of narrations. We ask Allah for protection. (K)

HIS APPOINTMENT AS JUDGE OF AL-RAQQA[68]

Abū Khāzim al-Qāḍī reported on the authority of Bakr ibn Muḥammad al-ʿAmmī that Muḥammad ibn Samāʿa said:

> The reason Muḥammad ibn al-Ḥasan was involved with the affairs of state was that Abū Yūsuf, the judge, was asked to recommend a man to be Judge of al-Raqqa, and said to them, 'I do not know of any suitable man but Muḥammad ibn al-Ḥasan; if you wish, then summon him from Kufa.' So they sent for him.
>
> When he arrived, he went to Abū Yūsuf and said, 'Why have I been sent for?' He said, 'They asked me to recommend a judge for al-Raqqa, so I suggested you. My intention behind this was that Allah has spread this knowledge of ours in Kufa, Basra and all the East, so I would love it to be in this area too, so that by your means Allah will spread our knowledge to it and to the lands of Syria beyond it.'
>
> Muḥammad replied, 'Glory to be Allah! Did I not deserve to be told first why I would be summoned?' Abū Yūsuf said, 'In any case, they have summoned you.' He told him to mount up, and he did so, and they set off and went to Yaḥyā ibn Khālid ibn Barmak. Abū Yūsuf said to Yaḥyā, 'Here is

68 Al-Raqqa is a town on the northern bank of the Euphrates, in modern-day Syria.

Muḥammad; do as you will with him.' Yaḥyā then continued to threaten Muḥammad until he accepted the post of Judge of al-Raqqa. This is how Abū Yūsuf and Muḥammad ibn al-Ḥasan fell out.[69]

Al-Ṭaḥāwī reported on the authority of Aḥmad ibn Abī ʿImrān that al-Ṭabarī heard Ḥumayd ibn al-ʿAbbās, who was one of the greatest companions of Muḥammad ibn al-Ḥasan, say, 'On Fridays, the circle in the mosque in Baghdad would be held by Bishr ibn al-Walīd. This went on, and we attended his circle there, until Muḥammad ibn al-Ḥasan came to town. After that, we would go to him and learn things from him, and then go to Bishr ibn al-Walīd and ask him

69 This was the reason for their temporary estrangement, and neither of them can be blamed for their part in it. As for what al-Sarakhsī relates at the beginning of *Sharḥ al-Siyar al-Kabīr*, it is a myth which entered his mind in his youth when he read it in some book of tales or another, and then dictated to his students when he was imprisoned and separated from his books.

The myth contradicts itself in several ways, because Muḥammad ibn al-Ḥasan was not in Baghdad until he was summoned, so it could not be the case that Abū Yūsuf was jealous of the number of Muḥammad's followers in the capital; moreover, a master is not jealous of his pupil's success, but rather he is proud of it. Add to this the fact that he was appointed Judge of al-Raqqa, where the caliphs had their summer residence, which would have brought him into very close contact with them – it was not the Judge of Egypt, as this myth has it! So it cannot be imagined that Abū Yūsuf recommended Muḥammad for the post because he wanted to remove him from the courts of the caliphs. There are other proofs of the falsity of the myth besides these, which I gave in full in my book *Bulūgh al-Amānī*. (K)

about them. This hurt him, and when he could bear it no longer he stopped holding the circle.'

Ibn Abī ʿImrān added that he heard Muḥammad ibn al-Ḥasan ibn Abī Mālik say:

> I saw Bishr ibn al-Walīd at my father's house, and he made a disparaging remark about Muḥammad ibn al-Ḥasan. My father said to him, 'Do not do that, Abū al-Walīd! Muḥammad has as much esteem with the people as all these books do. We would like it if you would accept the task of posing questions on our behalf; and Allah has relieved you of the burden of having to answer them.'

Al-Ḥasan ibn Abī Mālik is reported to have said about the scholarship of Muḥammad ibn al-Ḥasan, 'Even Abū Yūsuf did not go into such detail!'

Al-Ṭaḥāwī reported, on the authority of Muḥammad ibn al-Ḥasan ibn Mirdās, that Muḥammad ibn Shujāʿ said, 'Muḥammad ibn al-Ḥasan and his book *al-Jāmiʿ al-Kabīr* are like a man who builds a house, putting ladders between the floorsas he builds higher. Finally, when it is done, he comes down, takes out all the ladders, and says to the people, "There you are: climb!"'

Al-Ṭaḥāwī reported, on the authority of Abū Muḥammad ibn Salāma that Muḥammad ibn ʿAlī ibn Maʿbad ibn Shaddād reported that his father said:

> I went to al-Raqqa while Muḥammad ibn al-Ḥasan was the judge there. I went to his door

and asked leave to go in to see him, but I was not allowed in. I left, and stayed for some time in al-Raqqa without going to see him.

One day I was in the street when he came along on his mount, dressed in his judicial apparel. When he saw me, he approached me and asked me to slow down, and left someone with me to lead me to his house. When he got home and sat down, I was led in to him. He said to me, 'What has kept you away for so long? I heard that you were here.' I said, 'I came to see you, but was not allowed in.' This displeased him, and he said, 'Who kept you out?' I thought that he had a mind to punish the doorman, so I did not tell him. He said, 'If you do not tell me, I will do away with all of them!'[70] He summoned them all and said, 'You have no business barring Abū Muḥammad from me.'[71] From then on, I would go and visit him, approach the curtain and clear my throat and speak a greeting, and he would say, 'Come in.'[72]

70 Ibn Abī al-ʿAwwām adds here: 'I said, "Then you will do an injustice to those who did not bar me!"' (W)

71 Ibn Abī al-ʿAwwām adds here: 'He then looked at me and said, "When you come to us, there is nothing between me and you but the curtain which keeps people from me. Clear your throat there, or utter a greeting. If I am able to admit you I will do so myself; if I am unable, then I will keep silent, and you should go." After that, I would go to visit him and find people waiting at his door, and I would go past them and past his doormen, and head straight to the curtain.' (W)

72 Ibn Abī al-ʿAwwām adds here: 'Or else he would be silent, and I would leave.'

Al-Muslim ibn Muḥammad al-Qaysī and others informed me, on the authority of al-Yumn al-Kindī – ʿAbd al-Raḥmān ibn Muḥammad – Aḥmad ibn ʿAlī al-Ḥāfiẓ – Ibn Rizqūyah – Ibn al-Sammāk – Muḥammad ibn Ismāʿīl al-Tammār – Aḥmad ibn Khālid – al-Muqaddamī (in Basra), that al-Shāfiʿī said:

> Muḥammad ibn al-Ḥasan is still a great man in my eyes. I spent sixty dirhams on his books, and finally met him at Hārūn's court. He said, 'O Commander of the Faithful, the people of Medina have gone against the Book of Allah, the laws of the Messenger of Allah ﷺ, and the consensus of the Muslims.' I was sorely affronted by this, and said, 'Perhaps you mean the Prophetic Household! The grave of the Messenger of Allah ﷺ is in their midst, yet you attack them!'[73]

73 The 'Aḥmad ibn ʿAlī' in this chain of transmission is al-Khaṭīb al-Baghdādī, who drank intoxicants according to Yāqūt in *Muʿjam al-Udabāʾ* on the authority of al-Ḥāfiẓ ʿAbd al-ʿAzīz al-Nakhashī, and who was obsessed with seducing young boys and indulging in his scandalous desires according to several books by Ibn al-Jawzī and Sibṭ al-Jawzī, and also in al-Malik al-Muʿaẓẓam ʿĪsā al-Ayyūbī's *al-Sahm al-Muṣīb*, and elsewhere. We took him to account for his lies against the Greatest Imam, the Jurist of Islam, Abū Ḥanīfa al-Nuʿmān, in *Taʾnīb al-Khaṭīb*, and for his disrespect of Abū Yūsuf and Muḥammad ibn al-Ḥasan and others as well, citing clear evidences. Notice that he narrated a great many things from Ibn Rizqūyah after he had grown blind and infirm, which is something that only someone who found it easy to deceive the Muslims would do.

The 'Abū ʿAmr ibn al-Sammāk' in the chain is ʿUthmān ibn Aḥmad al-Daqqāq, who narrated outrageous things with chains of transmission

Ḥanbal ibn Isḥāq reported that he heard Aḥmad ibn Ḥanbal say: 'Abū Yūsuf was fair in Hadith; as for Abū Ḥanīfa and Muḥammad ibn al-Ḥasan, they were not

---

that are worthless even by al-Dhahabī's admission.
The character of the 'al-Tammār' in the chain is unknown, and he was never declared trustworthy, although al-Khaṭīb does give an entry for him in *al-Tārīkh*.
The 'Aḥmad ibn Khālid (al-Karmānī)' in the chain is also unknown.
In sum, this story is a lie against al-Shāfiʿī. Although he used strong words when debating, he was not the type of person to resort to putting false words in his opponent's mouth. It is curious how at one moment they report that Muḥammad ibn al-Ḥasan preferred Mālik to Abū Ḥanīfa in jurisprudence, and the next moment claim that Muḥammad said that Mālik did not have the right to give legal opinions. They take offence at the brilliant rebuttals he gave to Mālik in his book *al-Ḥujja ʿalā Ahl al-Madīna*, and try to make it seem that he was rebutting the Household of the Messenger of Allah ﷺ, and they mention the grave of the Prophet ﷺ and the Abode of Revelation, attempting thereby to prevent anyone from rebutting the errors made by the jurists of Medina!
What do the Prophetic Household, the Abode of Revelation and the Perfumed Grave have to do with rebuttals of Mālik and some of his shaykhs? Muḥammad ibn al-Ḥasan's rebuttals cannot be answered in this way; arguments must be met with arguments.
Whoever invented this story also did a disservice to al-Shāfiʿī. It is authentically narrated that al-Shāfiʿī studied jurisprudence with Muḥammad, and that he loaded his camel with books of his teachings. This childish abuse is not the way a student addresses his teacher; rather, it is the way of those who seek victory by any means, fair or foul. Far be it for al-Shāfiʿī to take such an approach! Moreover, al-Shāfiʿī's own rebuttal of Mālik in *al-Umm* is much harsher than Muḥammad ibn al-Ḥasan's rebuttals of Mālik in *al-Ḥujja*. All guidance comes from Allah. (K)

in accord with the tradition.'[74] Al-Dāraquṭnī said, 'In my view, Muḥammad does not deserve to be rejected.'[75] Al-Nasā'ī said, 'His hadiths are weak.'

As for al-Shāfiʿī (may Allah have mercy on him), he deemed the hadiths narrated by Muḥammad ibn al-Ḥasan strong enough to be cited as evidence for his arguments. We have it on the authority of ʿAlī ibn

74 The *mujtahids* differ widely regarding the criteria for the acceptability of a report: what one person accepts, another might reject because it falls short of his own criteria for acceptability. Every single imam has had things like this said about him, so this criticism does not amount to a great deal. (K)

75 Al-Dāraquṭnī, despite his very excessive disparagement of Abū Ḥanīfa and his companions because of his divergence from them on important matters of doctrine, as well as subsidiary matters of law, said in *Gharā'ib Mālik* when speaking about the narrations pertaining to the act of raising the hands when coming out of the bowing position in prayer: 'Twenty trusted *ḥāfiẓ* narrators reported it, including Muḥammad ibn al-Ḥasan al-Shaybānī, Yaḥyā ibn Saʿīd al-Qaṭṭān, ʿAbdallāh ibn al-Mubārak, ʿAbd al-Raḥmān ibn Mahdī, Ibn Wahb, and others.'

See, then, how al-Dāraquṭnī puts Muḥammad ibn al-Ḥasan at the head of this list of trusted *ḥāfiẓ* narrators, which is a clear testimony from him that he was a trusted *ḥāfiẓ*. Thus anyone who says of those who deem Muḥammad to be a gifted, most-able *ḥāfiẓ* that 'He is a one-eyed man among the blind' is himself a blind man among the one-eyed!

He was also declared trustworthy by Ibn al-Madīnī, as is stated in Ibn Ḥajar's *Taʿjīl al-Manfaʿa* and elsewhere. Al-Dhahabī said in *al-Mīzān*, 'Muḥammad ibn al-Ḥasan was an ocean of knowledge and jurisprudence, and strong in what he transmitted from Mālik.' If he was strong in transmitting what he heard from Mālik on isolated occasions, how could he not be strong in what he transmitted from his shaykh, after devoting his life to studying his teachings and narrations? Allah knows best, and all praise is to due to Him, and no other. (K)

Aḥmad al-Ḥāfiẓ and others, who heard it from: al-Ḥusayn ibn Abī Bakr al-Ḥanbalī – Aḥmad ibn ʿAbd al-Munʿim al-Qazwīnī – Muḥammad ibn Saʿīd al-Ṣūfī – Ṭāhir ibn Muḥammad al-Maqdisī – Makkī ibn Manṣūr – Aḥmad ibn al-Ḥasan al-Qāḍī – Muḥammad ibn Yaʿqūb – al-Rabīʿ ibn Sulaymān – **Muḥammad ibn Idrīs al-Shāfiʿī** – **Muḥammad ibn al-Ḥasan** – Qays ibn al-Rabīʿ – Abān ibn Ghālib – al-Ḥasan ibn Maymūn – ʿAbdallāh ibn ʿAbdallāh Mawlā Banī Hāshim – Abū al-Janūb al-Asadi, that ʿAlī 🕮 said, 'If someone is under our protection [*dhimma*], then his blood is like our blood, and his indemnity is our indemnity.'

Muḥammad ibn al-Ḥasan is said to have had great cleverness, intelligence and dignity, and to have recited the Qurʾan very often.

Al-Ṭaḥāwī reported, on the authority of Aḥmad ibn Abī ʿImrān, that one of the companions of Muḥammad ibn al-Ḥasan said, 'Muḥammad's regular daily and nightly recitation was one third of the Qurʾan.'

Abū Ḥāzim al-Qāḍī reported that he heard Bakr al-ʿAmmī say, 'Ibn Samāʿa and ʿĪsā ibn Abān learned their prayer from none other than Muḥammad ibn al-Ḥasan.'

Yūnus ibn ʿAbd al-Aʿlā reported, on the authority of ʿAlī ibn Maʿbad, that the man of Rey in whose house Muḥammad ibn al-Ḥasan died said, 'I went to see Muḥammad on his deathbed. He wept, and I said to him, "Do you weep, despite the knowledge that you have?" He replied, "Tell me: if Allah brings me before Him, what shall I say if He asks me, 'What brought you to Rey? The struggle in My cause, or the search for My good favour?'" Then he died, may Allah have mercy on him.'

Abū Khāzim ʿAbd al-Ḥamīd al-Qāḍī reported that when al-Rashīd buried Muḥammad ibn al-Ḥasan and al-Kisāʾī (in Rey), he recited the following verses:

I mourned Muḥammad, the Judge of Judges;
My tears flowed, and my heart sorrowed.
Then the death of al-Kisāʾi shocked me,
And the vast earth almost trembled under my feet.
They were two scholars who died and passed away,
And there is no one left in the world to match them.

Al-Sīrāfī said that the [following] lines were composed by Yaḥyā al-Yazīdī, and that the poem begins:

The world moves on, and does not last forever;
The splendour you see now will surely fade.
Every man must drink from death's cup,
Which will be passed to each one of us in turn.
Do you not see how old age heralds decay,
And that the bloom of youth does not return?
What did away with ages past will visit you, too;
So be well prepared: annihilation awaits.

Praise be to Allah, and no other.

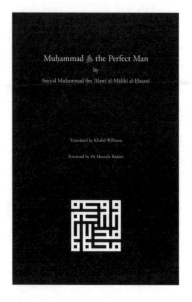

The Virtues of Imam Abū Ḥanīfa

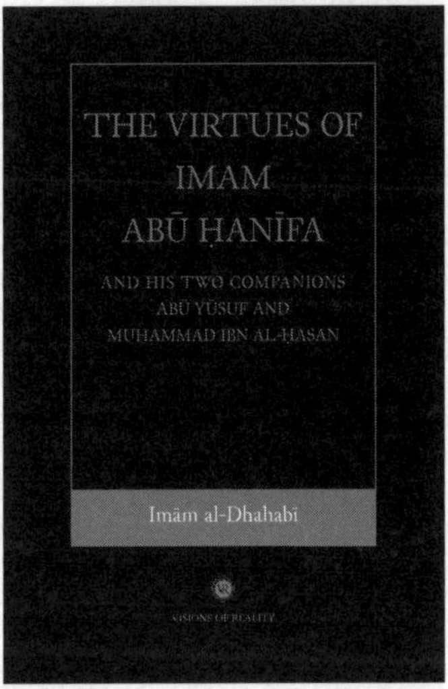

AL-IMĀM AL-AʿẒAM Abū Ḥanīfa was the founder of the madhhab that bears his name, which was given its fullest expression by his 'Two Companions', Imām Abū Yūsuf and Imām Muḥammad ibn al-Ḥasan. It is the largest of the four madhhabs and is most extensive in the East, but with a sizeable presence in Europe and the West with the presence of immigrant Turkish and Pakistani Muslim communities.

Imām al-Dhahabī was born in Damascus in 673 AH. Over 1,200 scholars transmitted hadiths from him via direct transmission and ijāza. His authored works amount to almost one hundred books. He was a man of noted intelligence and a renowned ḥāfiẓ. He continued to write until he lost his sight in the year 743, and died on the eve of Monday the 3rd of Dhul-Qaʿda, 748 in Damascus.

With extensive notes by Shaykh Abū al-Wafāʾ al-Afghānī (1310-1395AH) and Shaykh Muḥammad Zāhid ibn Ḥasan al-Kawtharī al-Ḥanafī al-Ashʿarī (1296-1371AH) this work will be indispensable to the serious student.

A Journey of Loving Hearts to the Master of Divine Envoys

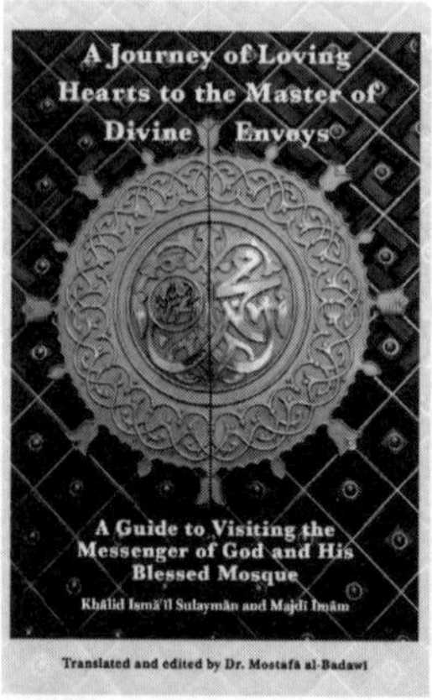

A Guide to Visiting the Messenger of God and his Blessed Mosque

This is the definitive guide to visiting the Messenger of God, may peace and blessings be upon him, with high adab and courtesy the book takes the visitor to the Radiant City of Madina, and the Blessed Mosque of the Messenger of God, and onwards through to presenting oneself in front of the Best of Creation ﷺ.

En route the authors dedicate chapters to The Merits of the Possessor of the Tremendous Character, the Shariah position of visiting him, Attributes of the City of the Messenger of God and his blessed Mosque, Recommendations for the Visitor of Madina the Radiant, Names of the Chosen One, The Good Manners in Standing in the Presence of the Chosen One, How to Visit the Beloved ﷺ.

This is a tremendous work which will be a valuable addition to the traditional Islamic literature in the English language.

The Sublime Truths of the Shādhilī Path

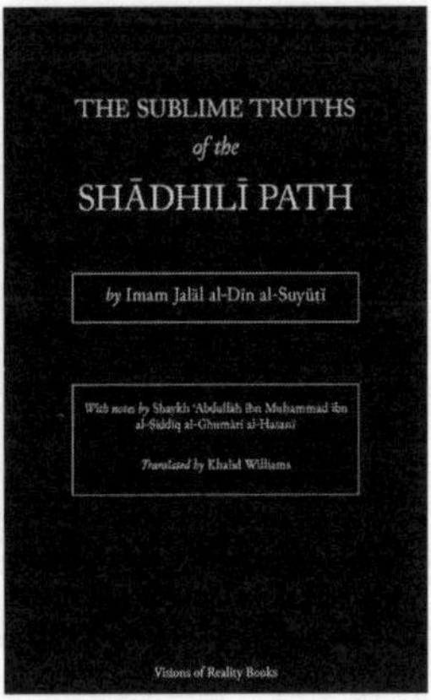

Shaykh Abū al-Ḥasan al-Shādhilī took the Path from Shaykh ʿAbd al-Salām ibn Mashīsh, who took it from Shaykh ʿAbd al-Raḥmān al-Madanī, and so on back one by one to al-Ḥasan ibn ʿAlī ibn Abī Ṭālib, the first *quṭb*. The reason why the shaykhs of the Path of Ṣūfī initiation have to be listed in this way is because it is a matter of transmission, and transmission requires a chain.

Shaykh Abū al-Ḥasan al-Shādhilī would be visited by scholars, such as Sulṭān al-ʿUlamāʾ Shaykh ʿIzz al-Dīn ibn ʿAbd al-Salām and Shaykh Taqī al-Dīn ibn Daqīq al-ʿĪd.

Abu'l-Faḍl ʿAbd al-Raḥmān ibn Abī Bakr ibn Muḥammad Jalāl al-Dīn al-Khuḍayrī al-Suyūṭī (born on the 1st of Rajab 849AH/1445, died in 911AH/1505) was a Shāfiʿī *mujtahid* Imam, Ṣūfī, ḥadīth master (*ḥāfiẓ*) and historian, and a prolific writer who authored works in virtually every Islamic science.

THE PERFECT FAMILY – VIRTUES OF THE AHL AL-BAYT

The Perfect Family – Virtues of the Ahl al-Bayt is an unparalleled work about the position of the people of the Sunna on the beloved family of the Messenger of Allah ﷺ.

With a foreword by Dr. Mostafa al-Badawi, it comprises Imam al-Suyūṭī's *Iḥyāʾ al-Mayt bi-Faḍāʾil Ahl al-Bayt* 'Reviving the Dead: the Virtues of the Prophetic Household', Ibn Shahīn's *Faḍāʾil Fāṭima,* Imam al-Suyūṭī's *The Radiant Smile – On the Virtues of Our Lady Fāṭima*, Imam an-Nasāʾī's *Khaṣāʾis Imam ʿAlī* 'The Unique Distinctions of ʿAlī', the chapters on *Faḍāʾil* and *Manāqib* of Ahl al-Bayt from *Ṣaḥīḥ al-Bukhārī* and *Sahih Muslim* with the commentaries of Imam al-Nawawī and Ibn Ḥajar al-ʿAsqalānī

Selection and composition of the text is by Amjid Illahi, and the work has been translated by Khalid Williams and edited by Mahdi Lock.